Me and Mr. Mephistopheles

Novels by D.D. Cross

Onions Bunions Corns and Dungeons

A Den of Brigands

Forheavenstake

Field of Corns

Devilzinthedetails

Hellitainteasy

Back to Hades: Eustice Seeney Returns to Hell

Go to Hell! (I DID): Interview With Eustice Seeney

Heapatrouble

Me and Mr. Mephistopheles

Me and Mr. Mephistopheles

D. D. Cross

MMA
Publishing

Who would rid the world of the Devil they know?

Preface

Please allow me to introduce myself: I am a master of the universe, the dark part that is. I have great wealth, fine taste, influence, power, and eons of wisdom at my disposal. My duty is to inspire humanity to remain in a state of flux, alter fate, and tempt the species to function with hate.

Few if any have terms of endearment for me. My domain is not a destination on any map, but a sentence shouted out in anger.

Throughout human history I have been the darkness to avoid. A caveman views a tiger and with a jolt of fear, the words he didn't holler had a meaning that was clear. "Oh Hell!" The terms had not been named, but their meaning all the same. It was me they cried out for, and my purpose was to blame. They knew me from the beginning, and many more they came.

Whatever wretched, rotten, or insane, some misery, cruelty, a broken heart or pain. The human race was ready with one more phrase or name. It is me they call out to with every newfound strain. As they age, decay, and rot, the humans fan my flame. I've offered choices all along to ease mankind's bane. What I want in exchange for service is their soul, and that's my gain.

I whisper in their minds. With each pressure, stress, or bill unpaid, the loss of something dear. The urgency or need to have, becomes to them so clear. I emerge to plant a seed, a thought, a plan, a scheme, an easy choice indeed. I ask only for what remains, any faith they have agreed. Some believe in nothing, and those souls become my own. The simple picking self contrived, in terms of Satan's tools. A challenge is the suffering soul, whose faith begets a dual. I introduce the concept if they'll make it through the day. My offer makes them ponder, wonder, and finally doubt, if something out there yonder will truly be about.

The souls who are most rigid I find to be a drudge. Despite my badgering presence it is they who will not budge. No matter how intense I get there are rules I must obey. Sometimes the words do form, and those say: "Stay away."

However, I never give up easily. I put nightmares in their dreams. For some make them lie awake. Worry is my ally, dread is my friend. A fury of feverish fantods follow my prey, especially when they try to get away.

ME AND MR. MEPHISTOPHELES

I persist when they are vulnerable and weak, and say words to ease their pain. Lies beautifully crafted. Delightful false hope. I speak softly, offering charmed solutions. Resolutions to make problems go away.

Many ponder what may come. Is there life beyond death? What will become of their eternal souls?

For eons the blasted religions have instilled these ideations of Heaven. It has caught on in so many versions, across so many cultures, it makes my work complex. This has not been unsurpassable.

666

1

Good and evil. For the masses that is all they know. My job is placing souls in an eternity, a place they've never seen. A locale without time, dimensions, air, water, or any physicality. A stretch of faith. Religions preach not to give in to my easy way out. Alas, I simply pose the fact it is a place they may not reach. The human is fragile, they often just give up. That dire diagnosis. Some beg and pray for a miracle, worry, fret, and crumble as their deities just stumble. An afterlife is no substitute for a very poor prognosis. All they must do is suspend their disbelief, and I step in with solutions, and always do deliver. For those who break my hold I must relinquish. My powers have all been spent.

Some have built monuments to represent me. As some awful character, with horns, a pitchfork, and surrounded by flames. Lord or Prince of Darkness, Satan, Lucifer, so many names I've actually lost track.

ME AND MR. MEPHISTOPHELES

Thankfully my smartphone can pull up the data if I need it. For Christ's sake, I am only a Master of The Universe. I have a job to do. I haven't had a vacation in five thousand years!

My job as the Devil isn't to steal souls, or eternally damn humans. No, not at all. People do that to themselves. I just provide choices.

In fact, you've done so well over the last few centuries its made my work ridiculously simple. Now with the internet? Please. I barely have to leave Hell.

Let's face it there is the man-made concept of good and evil, darkness and light. It goes way back to cave dwelling days when I had first dibs on you people. That was the simple part. Easy pickings when there weren't many rules imposed upon you. Shit, dragging some broad by her hair into a cave and having your way with her was no big fucking deal. Knocking off a sibling, nothing. Stealing? Who cared. Everything was just fine. Humans were just doing what the specs said: Human Physiology 101. The Creator of the Universe pretty much set the tone. My job wasn't particularly rough back then. After all there were no "rules engraved in stone," right?

Yes, it WAS that easy. Humans being what they are, fucked up so much that the Boss set out a guidebook. Rules and regulations, and pitted me against the rules. All I wanted was to tickle the back of their neck.

To urge them to look at a wreck. To linger on that picture of something naughty. To fan the flames of guilt. No big deal, right? Well, the centuries went on and the rules got more stringent. People began believing their natural instincts were foul, dirty, and the nature of my game: Evil. A little more difficult to discern, because there are exceptions to all rules. The nature of evil was, is, and will be perpetually debated. That doesn't change things. That won't alter the fact that people will continue to fuck other people up. Sounds simple, doesn't it?

I just wait. Maybe provide a door, a choice, a decision, and let `em rip. Real easy you'd think. It isn't. There have been some real thorns in my ass. I shall return to those thorns for the purpose of this discourse momentarily.

As humanity goes, the world of damnation was doing just so for a millennium. Then I had this burst of the internet giving me countless souls to deal with. Shit, Hell was the place to be. I couldn't keep up with the billions of corrupt human circuitry making their way into what some called home. My place that is: the Devil's Domain—HELL.

Here is my gripe: I'm sure you know there must be balance in the universe. Without Hell's counterpart, Heaven, humanity would be a bland bunch of people running around killing each other, fucking each other, and fucking each other over. Good vs Evil, one always wins out. Blah blah blah.

No good without evil. Good guys, bad guys, bear with me, I've been at this forever. I'm just doing my fucking job.

ME AND MR. MEPHISTOPHELES

Sending off the human soul to my place, Hell. Tempting those to make choices, to head my way. No big deal.

This was supposed to be the easiest gig in the universe. All things so they say, to an end must come. As such my reign in Hell has been put in jeopardy. I have been given a week's notice to make Hell more Hellish.

Why? A certain "douche bag" got in my shit. The Powers That Be have decided my work as ruler of Hades is less than adequate. I have become stagnant, and a restructuring of Hades is in order. Even my supercomputers have been outsourced. I pled my case to little avail. The Powers believe a far more heinous afterlife for violators is required, to maintain cosmic balance and sustain order. Egads, rumors of bringing in an alien have surfaced!

However, as the grand manipulator, the master of all earthly temptation, and mankind's calculus of corruption: I know that I can bring Hell back to its realm of dread and horror. Depravity, desolation, despair, and my favorite, desire. Ha. All the D's I have built into the minds of little people since they left the cave. I have placed the itch to be scratched, dangled the carrot, placed that earthly temptation within reach for all mankind. Alas it was me, my handiwork all along. Now back to this thorn, Eustice Seeney. I must discover how he managed to escape, and use his nuanced ways to build a better Hell. For this is the only route for me to impress upon The Powers That Be, to allow me to remain in my position.

I must therefore establish a line of communication with Seeney, and appeal to his sensibilities that my replacement could shift the earth's axis.

I shall embark upon a dialogue with the one man—an imbecile at that—who managed to get out of Hell twice, and get his sorry ass kicked out of Heaven too!

I shall have one of my minions deliver notice to Seeney with an offer he cannot refuse.

What man would rid the world of the Devil they know? I shall get his attention by tethering his frail ego. Ha.

LETTER FROM SATAN TO SEENEY

Dear Mr. Seeney,

It has come to my attention that you have been making a mockery of my domain. As you know, I have had the pleasure of your presence at my facility. The damage to Hades has been tremendous. Fortunately we are insured. In fact, we own all the insurance companies on your crappy planet. Nonetheless, you are besmirching our bad name by minimizing the magnitude of suffering we provide through your semi-humorous commentaries. We have arranged to continually keep them in obscurity.

ME AND MR. MEPHISTOPHELES

Feel free to continue complaining. However, as you know you are no longer welcome here. Also from reliable sources, it is my understanding you are not welcome in Heaven either. I may be relieved of my duties as the ruler of the underworld. As a result the Devil whom you know will be replaced.

Your guess is as good as any as to, whom, or what, will rule damnation.

In dark of this overhaul, humanity may very well be taken aback by a new regime in Hades. Consider the ramifications of an alien, or non-human in command. The massive revision of an eons tested hereafter could very well disrupt all mankind.

Sincerely yours,

Satan

PS: Please leave your response in your mailbox after midnight. This letter will destroy itself after reading.

2

EUSTICE SEENEY

Howdy Doody Folks. It's me Eustice Seeney. I reckon if you got this far you read that letter. You might be wonderin' iffen it's really from Satan and how I got it, right? I got me one of them mailboxes with one of those little red flags that go up and down, so the postman knows you got mail to go out, or if he's left somethin'. It looks like a birdhouse or little shack, and just about anybody could put somethin' in it, but that's a crime. The cops'd haul you into the station you go fussin' with that. But folks do anyhow. Heck, I once had some kids put a cherry bomb in there, pert near put my eye out. Collsarn kids these days.

I live at the end of a dead end street, on a cul-de-sac, in a little development. That's just right for folks who like it real private. My place is right up on the swamp, and I fancy havin' a whole bunch of nature all around.

ME AND MR. MEPHISTOPHELES

I got me more plants growin' around my crib than the jungle, on account this is South Florida. The Everglades is like some kind of park that's protected from folks like me.

I see signs sayin': "No Fishing," and I gotta wonder why. But that's not here nor there. I gotta tell you about this letter from Satan.

That there was the first letter, and it showed up some time in the middle of the night. I know this on account the little red metal flag was stood up, indicatin' somebody put somethin' in that box while I was sleepin'. I peeked out the front window, and the first thing I saw was that thing standin' there like a collsarn boner on a donkey. I got to wonderin' if it was a prank, or some hooky fanooki trick. That sort of stuff happens around these parts. I didn't have my coffee yet, and the collsarn notion that somebody did somethin' to my mailbox riled me up, so I didn't need no caffeine. Somethin' wasn't right, and I felt it. I knew I had to look into this, and it bugged me. I had the heebie-jeebies, and my hands was shakin' when I pulled on my thickest gloves. I felt sweat on my forehead as I pulled down the goggles. I was up to the full blown freak-out when I wrapped a real thick blanket around me in case it was another stinker from Satan.

I mustered up my courage, and pulled out a big ole envelope that had my name on it. It was writ on colored paper that looked like money or royal shit.

It had some kinda seal made outta wax, or who knows what. Maybe somebody's guts, or the stuff they put in hot dogs?

I broke the seal and pulled out the letter. The envelope fell to the ground and burst into flames. I knew then that this wasn't some prank, and it sure was not of this earth. I stared at the letter, and had a general idea of who it was from. Ain't never seen anything like it. Maybe looked like a Bearer Bond like you see in the movies, and who knows it could've been writ in blood. At that moment I knew that this was a letter from none other than Mr. Mephistopheles. Collsarn rascal must've had one of his minions deliver it. Glad I ain't got return postage to pay.

3

I AM PEN PALS WITH SATAN

I thought this through, and fired off a letter fast. I knew Satan'd gotten lazy, and reckon he may've hit that glass ceiling. So I done writ.

Here goes. I put this on the envelope: From Eustice on my good Watermark Paper. Please don't go rippin' this up.

Dear Mr. Mephistopheles,

I read your letter, and do not feel but for nothing about your evil ways. I have told many people about that place you run. Not only is the service crummy, the cell phone connections suck, and basic cable is crappy.

So there.

I will continue to remind people of your rotten tricks and temptations. The simple fact is, that you put doors in front of people and give `em the key. That key bein the evil thoughts you put in their thinker brains. Yep, you get `em thinkin' evil thoughts using your hibbidy jibbidy satanical powers, and make them rely on their naturalized human stuff. They get to thinkin' and have to make decisions. And you, Mister Mephisto, nudge them. That there—the nudging bit—is against the cosmic rules, and I, Eustice Seeney, have filed a complaint with your supervisor. So in the meantime, Fuck you.

Sincerely,

Eustice Seeney

Note: Hoowee, I got me letters from Ole Mister Mephistopheles, that trickster sumbitch. I'm gonna play along with that old devil, and get some of my pals to jerk that rat basserd around. Lesson 1. Never trust the Devil. I don't rightly know what the next lesson is, but sure ain't gonna get conscriptuated to work for nothin'. Hell no.

* * *

DEAR MR. SEENEY,

I may be leaving Hell soon, and my replacement may have powers beyond my own. It is likely the rulers of Hades will be under new management. This means that once I am outsourced, who or what controls damnation may have powers beyond the Hell you know.

It is imperative that we communicate. As an escapee your insight into Hades, from a human point of view, might preclude such reorganization. You know my powers on earth are limited to influence, fear, temptation, and other means of corruption. NOT physical violence. However, under new management one never knows. Nonetheless, since you are among the living, it is outside my scope of demonic privilege—for now—to comport myself as the Hebrews say: a mensch.

Satan

* * *

Dear Satan,

I am referrin' these letters someplace on up. I am not telling you where neither. So there, you stinker.

Mr. Eustice Seeney

4

MEMORANDUM FROM THE DESK OF SATAN

For your information:

As the ruler of the underworld I am a busy entity. There's always something to deal with. Whether it's a crowding situation in one of the stadiums for folks with low FICO scores, or the parade of newbies not quite sure why they're damned. I've got to come up with a new introduction speech for each epoch.

The internet's been fine. However, I can't be bothered with the very twisted humans who've gone out of their way in heinous acts. I just pluck out their soul, and shove it in one of our offshore accounts. Oh my, the notion of an offshore account for the cosmos may be difficult to explain. Let me simplify it. Some souls are so revolting I have to send them off to one of my alien counterparts. An insect form of life that views mankind the way humans look upon ants. Some things are even too revolting for me. Bleah.

ME AND MR. MEPHISTOPHELES

So please keep in mind there may be a future in some insect Hell for you if you really step through a door. Face it I just put the doors up, YOU choose to enter. Did you ever watch bugs fuck? Think about getting it up the ass for eternity by some giant spider or fly. Some afterlife, huh?

I put in an order to ship Eustice off to some alien world, but even WE have rules. If your transgression is within human scope, the Hell has to remain consistent with the sin. Use your imagination it's a big mother fucking universe.

Eustice Seeney doesn't fit into that realm. He's just fucking with me by disseminating tales of the afterlife! That's nobody's business on earth while they're living. So the punishment fits the crime. It has to be this way or I lose my job, and some putz takes over. You'd be amazed at how many people want to be the Prince of Darkness.

* * *

DEAR MR. SEENEY

After careful consideration your requests are denied. There is no place in Hell for you.

Satan

* * *

DEAR SATAN,

What in tarnation sort of hibbidy jibbidy, riffraff, collsarn bull-pucky, is that? I don't want to go back to Hades. The place smelled from unwashed crotch, beer soaked bar rags, armpits, and burritos. The food was crummier than cardboard. Veggie burgers made from shoe leather? Non-alcohol beer? That there service at the Hades Bar sucked. The bartender had a piss poor attitude, and I'm right fine happy I didn't leave that sumbitch no tip. Fuck him. You can take Hell and shove it up your collsarn eternal damnated rectum.

Have a nice day,

Eustice

* * *

Dear Mr. Seeney,

What a delightful exchange. I will take your criticism's under advisement. However, the nether regions are in fact my domain, and I shall do with them as I see fit. The aromas of the damned serve a purpose, and we always strive for the finest foul odors all creation has to offer. With respect to your culinary complaints, may I remind you that dead people have no digestive systems.

Implying that our food is of a less than satisfactory quality is not only incorrect and unfounded, it is patently false. We have however, added alcohol to our beverages in Hell's combined waiting room and bar. As a token of our bad faith we will be sending along complimentary Hell Beer for you and a guest. As you know there is no place in Hell for you.

Respectfully,

Satan

P.S. Please be mindful that the bartender has two children to put through bad guy school.

5

RETURN MAIL

Dear Mister Mephistopheles,

I was just in Detroit. Hell cannot hold a candle to crummy places on earth. So there. In fact, getting dead twice and going to Hell was not as crappy of a trip than my last one to the Motor City, and then Cleveland.

If eternal damnation is spending eternity in your place there sure's heck got to be a lot of folk who ain't but never been to them cities. I would rather spend a few months in Hades than those towns. I have to reckon there are crummier parts of the world here. You would think if you was a bad person and died there'd be some rotten afterlife.

Hell is a predictable place. And that is why you trickster, nobody here on earth gets it. The it is this, Hell is just the same old shit every day for all time. For some people that is just a regular life. You are one dummy for the boss of the after world.

ME AND MR. MEPHISTOPHELES

Farthermuch, I got to tell you that all the scariness of going to Hell was made up by dummies. There weren't no infernos or fires. Just a bunch of stinky, pasty skinned, dead folks, walkin' around with no idea they was damned. Like I said, your neck of the woods ain't but for nothin' compared to some parts of `Merica.

Respectfully,

Eat Poo,

Eustice

* * *

MEMORANDUM FROM HADES

To: Eustice Seeney

From: The Desk of Satan

Please be advised your suggestions will be taken under consideration.

6 6 6

What the Hell sort of bull-pucky was that? Hellfire. I was sittin' in my kitchen sippin' a brew, listenin' to the TV, readin' this bullspit from Hell, and I got me a right ticked off. I set myself to writin' back.

* * *

Dear Satan,

Answer your own mail you collsarn sumbitch. Just on account you're too lazy to make Hell Hellish and spooky ain't my fault. Haven't you had to sit through crummy movies? I left two times, and it tweren't that hard. On account everything about Hades was el-cheapo. Your tricks were tricky and all, but the place looked like out of date shit from Disney, or some other theme park. Folks ain't so scared of stuff like that no more. You need to find some video game designers, or horror movie makers, to make your corner of the universe scarier. As an aside, I was also in Heaven, and that wasn't no big shake either. Everybody just floated around like zombies. I have only to reckon that regular life offers crappier things than Hell, and more cool things than Heaven. I will be taking this up with your boss.

You're friend,

Eustice Seeney

6

That's about when it occurred to me: that bein' dead ought just be some big ole long goodbye to your corporeal body. Why? That collsarn thing just rots and rots as you get older. Hell is pretty much the aging process of human bodies, and Heaven is the reverse. There's plenty of crumminess on earth, and good stuff too. I reckoned then that I could do me right well by gettin' my old pal Doc Wiley and a few other folks together, and set up a club or organization about the bull-pucky of Heaven and Hell.

Just like that it occurred to me: Satan and the Boss was conspirin' to make life itself one big afterlife. I know it don't make no sense on account the cost of livin' was up, and every day you wake up feeling crummier and crummier. Life itself is a little bit of Heaven and a little bit of Hell. In the final end of things you go to Heaven or Hell, but there ain't no big difference in the two.

On account they is both the same in their eternal, same old, shitedness. Hellfire, I had me a new mission.

* * *

DEAR MR. SEENEY,

This is an awkward letter, so please find a moment to consider my request. I was recently informed by The Powers That Be that I must visit earth in order to maintain my Satanic status, and licensure for galactic evil. In order to do this I will require an authentic human body to inhabit for a designated period of time, and lodging. As you most certainly know I have visited earth in the past using a composite shell, constructed solely for specific purposes. It is imperative that I go "fully human" to conduct the aforementioned mission proscribed by The Powers. Would you kindly help accommodate me? My employer will reimburse you for any expenditures, and since I am The Prince of Darkness you will enjoy some of the perks that come along with such title.

Always trying to make Hell more Hellish,

His Satanic Majesty,

Lewis Sifer

* * *

ME AND MR. MEPHISTOPHELES

EUSTICE

What in tarnation was that about? I tell you I ain't seen but for nothin like this one before. A collsarn doozy of a letter from that rascally Satan himself. I reckon he done got hisself in some trouble. On account last time I escaped from Hades he'd already started buildin' the place up like a theme park. I'm gonna have to call on my good ole pals to find out what to do.

* * *

7

TRIP WILEY, M.D.

Hello. I was Eustice's attending physician the three times he died—yes, 3's the charm. Eustice however, not so charming. He sent along the previous exchange of letters he's been saving. I asked myself what sort of nincompoop is pen pals with the Devil? I don't think I needed an answer. I will take this under advisement.

I've got to run someone's calling.

Trip

* * *

8

EUSTICE: DOC WILEY NEEDED TO SEE THIS.

Hellfire. I wrote Ole Doc Wiley, and sent him them letters from Satan. I know I could use the internet, but let me tell you this: That there is Satan and his minions playground. Hellfire, everything you type in goes into Satan's super duper computer, and he has the automated damnamator thingamajig. So I gotta be careful. I write back and forth with Ole Mister Mephistopheles on account of me bein' the only fella that escaped his clutches twice, and I secretly think he wants to know how. I'm cool with that. But when it comes to earthly stuff, I keep my emails to a minimum, and stay off that social media stuff too. That's why I sent this on over to the Doc.

What if I did put the old devil up, and hang out with Satan for a spell. Maybe I'd get me a glimpse into the ways of evil, and set out to neutralize some of the evil in the world. I'd call the Doc but all the phone lines are intercepted by Satan's minions too. I'll just wait till I hear back. I gotta go check my mail. You never know.

It occurred to me that Satan ain't gotta pay postage. I gotta find out how he does that? Maybe there's some minions workin' over to the post office. Hmm—maybe that's why my magazines get all smelly and crinkled up. I'll look into it.

* * *

Dear Satan,

I thunk about your askin' to come to earth and hang out. I don't know what kinda body I can find you, but gotta think about it. Do you wanna be a gal? I have an ex-wife that'd fit right well.

Eustice

* * *

Dear Eustice

Thank you for your kind offer. However, I will have to decline your body selection. I do not think that I would like to occupy the body of your ex-wife. There are things of the earth which are beyond revulsion even to me.

ME AND MR. MEPHISTOPHELES

I will find the appropriate body to inhabit, and look forward to my stay. Will advise upon my arrival.
I look forward to your hospitality.

Sincerely,

Satan

* * *

Eustice Notes:

Hellfire I got to have Satan come stay with me? Holy shit. I gotta do some checkin' to see if this is some sin or somethin'. I'm gonna have talk to some holy folks. I best wait till Doc Wiley finds out and maybe he'll help me out.

* * *

DEAR MISTER SEENEY,

I will be arriving on earth shortly, and have a few simple requests prior to my arrival. I will be staying at your home. Please refrain from playing Country Western music, and turn down the volume of the TV commercials. They are infuriating, and give Hell a bad name. Furthermore, I do not know what sort of body I will be occupying yet, and it may have certain dietary requests. Please find enclosed a Hades Express Card good at any earth merchant.

You're future houseguest,

Satan

* * *

I stopped readin' and crumpled up the letter. Satan's comin' over to visit? What am I sposed to do, messy up the place? Well I do have this nifty charge card, so I reckoned a good ole shoppin' trip'd be in order. I had to write that old devil back.

* * *

Dear Mister Mephistopheles,

My arm hurts from writin' all this shit. I am looking forward to hanging out with you. Please don't get me in any trouble with John Q. Law. Then again, if you got super duper powers that shouldn't be no problem. I reckon you got a lot of pals on the inside of most jails. I figure you might want to see how the humans have made

ME AND MR. MEPHISTOPHELES

Hell look like some sissy shit. I guess that you are coming here to check out how humans have really progressed.

My pal Doc Wiley said there ain't been no devil sightings on earth in a long time. But Jesus has been here a few times, as well as other good guys.

I will get a bunch of movies and some computer shit for you to fuss around with. Hoowee, you'll see that most of earth is filled with sinners and all. I don't reckon you wanna go to no war zones, on account you'll be in a human body and that'd make you real vulnerable to gettin' hurt. Hmm, just thinkin' about it. There might be some folks that'd want to beat the crap out of you, present company excluded. Cause you know I done whooped your ass a few times. So don't bother tryin' no devil tricks with some muscle pansy body. Oh yeah, that inhabiting bodies of my friends trick, nope. Don't do that. I have a Satan sniffin' dog that'll smoke your sorry Satanic tuchas out, and I reckon that wouldn't be good for your job.

That brings me to this: I figure that your career as the leader of Hell is on the line, and you have to figure out a way to make Hell bad again. So don't be a dick head, and maybe I'll help you rearrange the Universe. Like I said, Heaven ain't all it's cut out to be.

Oh yeah, have one of your minions get you a driver's license.

Your former arch nemesis.

9

SATAN'S RUMINATION

I was around when every crisis in human events transpired. Tempting mankind with evil, and building Hades upon man's darkest ideations. The fact that The Powers That Be have found Hell less than horrible is an insult. Where exactly do you place the developers of horror movies, authors of vampire books, and glamorized versions of war and suffering?

In the thousands of years I have ruled the netherworld, no period of mankind has been as unfazed about the horrors of eternal damnation. Humans have come to enjoy evil more than decency. Any self-respecting Prince of Darkness would be proud of this conversion. All things evil into the banal mundane of life. Those are things to experience for all eternity, not on earth, not as entertainment, not as a spectacle. Good demons? I am going to have to find out just what makes humans tick these days.

ME AND MR. MEPHISTOPHELES

The material I have been monitoring IS horrible. Traditionally these earth people should have been pilloried in the least for these transgressions. No more.

Something more rotten than what I have in Hell exists on earth, and is used as entertainment? Not in a million years. Now my career is on the line. The Big Guy and the forsaken Powers That Be. Curse them! I clench a symbolic fist and raise it to the Heavens. Heavens, Ha. I have been threatened. If I fail I will no longer have a place among the cosmology of this universe. I could be remanded to some court of some galaxy or dimension beyond even I can imagine. To stand trial and perhaps be summarily dispatched, rendered obsolete, a quick kill. Efficiently removing any and all remnants of the Hades I created! No. This is surely reprehensible. They are after all, The Powers That Be. If I am indeed found to be blameworthy for an inadequate afterlife for the little people: I—The Devil—must indeed pay my due. How dreadful. What if they send me back to earth in the form of some decrepit wench, pandering to the very scum I taunt? In the squalor of some inner city like L.A., or Miami? Oh myself!

No way out. I cannot refuse.

I must prepare myself. Alas, time to leave my slumber and delineating ways, and redecorate, redesign, and rebuild Hell, with the worst humanity has created. I will assemble my best minions for research. Egads, I am at least fifty earth years behind.

Perhaps I was asleep at my job. I did allow some escape. For one, there was no excuse as his fame grew. Odysseus, or as the tribal humans refer to in Latin, Ulysses. Son of Laertes, ruler of the island kingdom of Ithaca. I had Odysseus in my clutches. That buffoon grew to fame among the little people in his "Dante's Inferno," Canto 26. Absurd tales of the bottom of Hell. Imagine a human naming MY DOMAIN.

His lovely bride, Penelope, knitted and sewed as Odysseus schtupped and toyed with temptation. MY temptresses, before coming to MY HOME. Glamorizing this absurd tale as fact for centuries. That Ulysses-Odysseus languished in an eighth circle of Hell. Ah, Homer's Yarn went far beyond my warnings. Meant to instill fear. Some even claiming MY work for his success in that silly Trojan War. A child could have seen that one. OUTRAGEOUS how my domain has been ridiculed, speculated upon, and studied. Stupid, silly, wasteful humans.

There are NO circles of Hell. There are rings. The ridiculous notion of the "Divine Comedy," taken by the humans as fact. Ah, so revolting. Dante explains Ulysses presence in a "section" of Hell. That fool could not know of my home's chambers. Finally pronouncing that he was the only person ever to return from Hell alive. Bah. Nonsense. I let him go. I had no use for him. He was a tool, a ploy to spread my word to awaiting fools. I knew that would raise to acclaim, and be the subject of study for eons. It gave me time to enjoy my regal place as Lord Ruler of The Underworld.

Then came Seeney. A bumbling backwoods imbecile. Escaping the afterlife and eternal damnation, not just once, but TWO TIMES. For this nincompoop I must pay. Three strikes the PTB call it. Three strikes Satan, and we bring in our own version of all that terrifies humanity. I will destroy every Ingram of Seeney's being to find what lies beneath that hero, who is really a pusillanimous bumpkin. A weak-spirited, faint-hearted, timorous fool. I will discover the flaws which evolved in my system, and show The Powers that I AM the MASTER of all the bumps that go in the night. I am the horror awaiting the foul deeds they have done with their lives. But Seeney, that midget among giants, holds a key. A key that will be soon my own. Ha.

Lucifer.

I must send Seeney a note.

BEFORE LEAVING HELL FOR MY STAY AMONG HUMANS

Dear Eustice,

Over the years I have visited and inhabited several bodies, none of which beyond a few of your earthly days. I've always retained my own powers, never having to use such bodies for their intended purpose, life in general. I merely used them for whatever my mission required.

I have some familiarity with the pleasure portions, but not real working awareness of the flaws. I am shopping for the most comfort, least upkeep, and all around practicality. So far I have been baffled at how uncomfortable they all are. It bewilders me why the female version, especially the younger ones, require so much upkeep. Their minds filled with crippling concerns that are absurdly useless. The makeup, undergarments, and body parts, although curious, I would prefer leaving. Perhaps using one of the younger male versions instead, simply to put the penis in them. That penis thing on the males is a very odd appendage. In some males it can be used for several purposes, many of which I have damned folks for. Some are flat out ridiculous. It amazes me that the Creator of The Universe made this up. Please advise if the advent of modern cocksmanship is some sort of joke. The practical use of urinating is fine, the placing of it in the female vagina refreshing. I can see why some of the other penis uses are odd and damnable. Oh yes, tits on females? Although fun to play with, I do not enjoy having to wear a harness, and as they age the mushy texture is akin to rotting fruit. The vagina is a most curious body part that bleeds every month up to a certain age, and requires considerable upkeep.

Overall, you humans have shit choices for me in terms of which gender to inhabit for my earthly stay. Oh yes, the whole urination and defecation business is a real hassle. You will have to define the proper use upon my arrival. I think I will go with a younger version, with a functional penis so I can fuck some human females.

ME AND MR. MEPHISTOPHELES

Fraternally human to be,

Satan

* * *

I read that and had to just shake my head. Satan, he don't know shit about bein' human. Collsarn Satan's ain't never wiped his ass, and he wants to come visit? Dumbshit devil thinks he's gonna squeeze me. I'm gonna have to just think on this. So I send him back a note.

Memo to Satan:

Good luck with that, Mr. Mephistopheles. Ain't no human body gonna have what you're lookin' for, that ain't got no other prollems.

PS: If you don't like my spellin' go to Hell. PSS: Nix that, you already are in Hell.

I reckon I gotta get in touch with some old pals that know about this, so's I done left some messages. I started out with Doc Wiley.

10

TRIP WILEY MD

There was an urgent message on my voicemail. Seeney. Fucking Eustice Seeney.

Eustice is at it again, shit. He'll never just leave well enough alone. He could have just let things be, but no. Now, he needs ME. He needs my help with whatever miserable hurricane of hassle, hosting Satan is going to blow in. Fuck Fuck Fuck. I'm busy. Finally, back to doing some medicine, not full time, but at least I'm doctoring. I've got a life here, relationships, and my gig doing Elvis shows. Damn I just got my Elvis Tribute Card. I'll write him. If I call he'll just finagle me into one bullshit thing or another, and I can't let him. Not now. I have a life here. Maybe he can wrangle this himself.

11

EUSTICE GETS THE MAIL

The next day I saw the little flag on my mailbox had been put up. There was a letter. I had to reckon it was from Satan. Collsarn sumbitch.

Dear Eustice,

Alas, the time has whence come where I shall disembark my domain to walk among earth's people. Under guidelines set forth by such Creator of this Universe, I have been found—erroneously nonetheless—less than worthy to reign over Hell. I have been duly notified to relieve my command, and be remanded to some mortal flesh to walk among the creatures to be damned. I have been notified that if I fail at this odious task: of discovering new ways to make the human condition more foul than it is, and cultivate a hereafter of a more heinous experience, I will be cast to the farthest reaches of the universe to shovel space turds.

I certainly hope you have made preparations for my arrival, and arranged a tour of your miserable life, so I can get back to running Hell.

Your friend and perpetrator on probation of Hell,

Satan

P.S. Please stock up on Nacho Cheese Doritos. Although I have not chosen a body style all seem to favor this earthly delight.

* * *

NOTE TO SATAN:

Get your own collsarn food.

Eustice

* * *

DEAR MR. SEENEY,

This note is to apprise you of my preparations to take holiday on earth. Perhaps referring to my visit as a casual one will make for a more meaningful experience. As I mentioned in previous correspondence, the question of a suitable body is an issue. I am conducting research

40

among earth's finer penal institutions. Therein reside my largest population of allies, disciples, and damned. Sadly they are of little use regarding my task at hand. Ha. I certainly cannot use the body of a human who is already in Hell's registry, and you people already have persons well documented. I could hardly enjoy my visit in some rattle trap, marked, vehicle of flesh now could I? Double Ha. Be that as it may I shall make do.

I suspect you are aware that my visit is not entirely social, and my career as Lord of the Underworld is in jeopardy. Hell has been found by my superiors to match some of earth's expected unpleasantries.

I have been trying on male bodies, as I noted the female form is too much upkeep. And of late the age of the bodies seems to be a deciding factor, as well as the various disease states. I most certainly will need a body repairman, perhaps several, upon arrival. A pit crew so to speak. Ha. I believe I am acquiring some human humor. I suggest you summon your friend Doctor Wiley as he is familiar with your unique situation, to advise on this expedition and your part in it. I shall notify you once a suitable healthy human form is discovered for me to occupy.

Sadly my body choices for this particular visit are limited. Many potential bodies are unavailable—despite a willingness to sacrifice their life prematurely, but I am not permitted that luxury.

For all practical purposes I will require a body near its expiration date. An innocent, no family to miss them, no worldly issues or legal problems, no one in any of earth's databases. Certainly not a terrorist, or politician—amusing the similarities. Although a movie star would be what you people call "fun," that would hardly be in order. Maybe next time, if there is a next time, and no criminals! The awkward position of obtaining a driving or weapons permit would be limitless. That doesn't even factor in the ridiculous tattoos and piercings. Ha. So much for that notion.

Earth certainly has a wonderful array of motor coaches. I have been following the new BMW's and Audis and would appreciate your opinion, and perhaps the courtesy of renting one for me can be extended? Of course you will be handsomely reimbursed. By the way, is that new Lexus coupe comfortable for the human body? It looked very stylish in a movie I saw it in?

This morning I tried on the body of a male, aged fifty something, and must say it felt quite uncomfortable. The extremities were difficult to use, and the colored ink seemed rather alarming to other humans. Nonetheless, I do not understand this whole shaving and crapping procedure. Looking forward to my visit.

Your future houseguest,

Satan

* * *

ME AND MR. MEPHISTOPHELES

DEAR SATAN,

You are one collsarn moocher, you know that? Hellfire. I gotta get you a doctor too? What the heck kind of devil are you? Your letters make it seem like you are going to be getting a crummy body on this visit. It seems like you are going to be needing a whole pit crew on account this little journey of yours seems like a marathon, or an Earthionapolis 500.

I know I know you only got Chiropractors in Hell. But that Satanic Credit Card only goes so far, and you are askin' me for a whole lot. Doctors is doctors here in the US, and they got laws and rules. You know that. Sounds like you are tryin' to conscript me as a minion, and I will not join the forces of evil. Get your minions to do that you stinkpot.

Also, there ain't a whole lotta places take that Hades Card. I reckon that for the right price I can get Ole Doc Wiley to lend a hand with whatever body you nab. Just don't get one with them Nazi tattoos, on account that'll likely get you whooped real bad. And Doc Wiley ain't gonna keep prescribin' pain pills to you. Oh yeah, don't go gettin' a body of some famously bad crook like that Manson guy, or a killer or nothin'. On account the real estate values in my neighborhood are already crummy.

Oh yeah, what do you eat besides junk food, deviled eggs?

That was a joke, Satan. Get used to it, there's plenty of `em here.

Eustice

12

SATAN'S LOG

That nincompoop Seeney is going to be a challenge. I am dreading this earthly visit. The Powers That Be have certainly made this challenge vexing. Limiting my choices of body type to, "only pre-damned" humans. In fact, they must be at, or very near, their time of death. Why can't I just get a movie star body and face? So much for that if I want to keep my job and not be replaced by some computer program, or an alien from some star system that has no television or internet connections. Egads. This will have to be done. Shit. Fucking humans. Of all the lousy, rat bastard, temptable, little people I have to deal with, Seeney? Shit. Hell sure isn't what it used to be. Between that asshole and the Twilight Series —making the undead cool—really stuck in my cosmic craw. I am going to have to develop some super compartment of Hell for the "horror for amusement" folks. Maybe force them to sit in a room with Seeney for a few centuries. That is IF I still have a job. Hmm, I may be onto something to make Hell more Hellish. I suspect that

I must make the best of this trip. Off to earth in search of a halfway decent body. I have not told Eustice yet, but he will have to dispose of the body when I am done with it.

6 6 6

EUSTICE

Ole Doc Wiley didn't get back to me right quick, so I gave him another ringin' up.

I called up Doc Wiley again and tole him about the money. I'd have to reckon that if Ole Mister Mephistopheles was gonna be comin' to earth usin' someone's body, he'd sure's fire need a doc. I had to reckon Ole Doc Wiley, my good friend, and a fella familiar with the afterlife and all that hibbidy jibbidy stuff, havin' him a prescription pad'd come in right handy. You never know what sort of hellacious cooties Satan'd bring along with him. Let's face facts folks, that expression: When the Devil comes knocking on the door, somethin' or other, blah blah blah?

Well, I know that expression, and your good buddy Eustice ain't lettin' no demon in his collsarn door without bein' preparated. I gotta reckon ole Satan's gonna have his minions, cronies, and all sorts of bull-pucky evil folks, to help `em out in badnessness. Ole Doc Wiley'd be right good with a hypodermic needle, put that human form of

ME AND MR. MEPHISTOPHELES

Satan in a tizzy lickety-split. I don't reckon I gotta clean up the place or nothin', on account Satan's pickin' up the tab. You see, he can't stay at no hotels on account of all them screweillance video cameras and stuff. I don't reckon that'd fit his Satanical plans.

Now I gotta take pause here and explain to you: Ole Eustice is no dummy when it comes to givin' folks real life tours of dangerous places. Hellfire, I'd been an airboat tour guide for years, wrestled gators, been dead and went to Hades, and I went to the place up there in the clouds too. You might say that I been kicked outta more places than most folks ever knew was.

Let me tell you a might bit about my home:

I got me a nice spread at my favorite mobile home park. Collsarn biggest spread out of `em all, right there on the edge of the swamp. Everglades that is. Ole Satan steps outta line there's plenty of bull gators out here that'd chomp him into nothingness.

I got it all figured as to why Satan's comin', and my sources confirm it. Satan's Hell is like the Stuckey's on the turnpike. It just ain't too spooky, and the food ain't too good. The fact remains that most of life on earth is pretty shitty for most folks, and Satan ain't never really lived life as a person.

Nope, he ain't been in human form for any real spell, and no way he's gonna get it. I know Satan's visited here and there, sampled some goodies and all, but doubt real serious iffen he ever done any sufferin'. I know the Devil, and he ain't one to take no crumminess, spoilt basserd he is. Therefore, I think settin' him up for a real human experience'd do him some good, in that bad sort of way. This way I won't be playin' nurse maid to the chief of the forces of evil. But make for a world of pain worser and worser than what folks like me—folk'd been to Hell—already know. I have to reckon I can get me some help too. I know Doc Wiley'll be able to sick him up a bit. He got friends too. Give Mr. Mephistopheles a taste of good ole human sufferin'.

Now I gotta be double sure that what I am about to get myself involved in ain't no sin or nothin'. Aidin' and abettin'? Hmm, I rapped with a lawyer about that, and since Satan's an intellectual construct he ain't more than an idea. Bein' in America you're allowed to mess around with free speech, I think. So I'm not sure if I'm covered there. But we're talkin' about eternity and cosmic stuff, so I'd have to reckon the laws of nature and man don't right apply beyond this corporeal world, right?

Now dependin' on the body Satan uses—I ain't got no say in that—iffen he has a convicted criminal body Hellfire, I can't hang with him. That'd make me an accessory. And I, Eustice Seeney himself, could get myself hornswoggled into some criminal fandango. That there'd be when the laws of mankind kick in.

I seen them laws kick in with them terrorists and all. I could land my good ole corporeal self over to the

Guantanamo . . . Mm-hmm, I gotta be real careful Satan don't go gettin' mixed up with that bunch of troublemakers. They give humanity itself a bad name.

I best get to writin' Satan, and tell him he best find a legit body that's not a criminal. I sure's Hell don't want my neighbors freakin' out either, and I got me some doozies too. Last thing I need is for that cranky drunk Elmo Bazzer, the retired postman, actin' up. He's liable to cause a stir.

The more I think about this, the more hinky and complicated it's gettin'. Maybe gettin' himself the body of somebody close to dyin', and REALLY show Satan what human sufferin's about. If I do that it'd make the state of bein' human a realistical view, and the Big Guy wouldn't be ticked off. If the job here is for Hell to be more Hellish the sake of makin' humans be more humane to other humans so's they don't do bad things, that'd be a good deed.

I reckon the whole purpose of this is to make humanity more humane altogether. And if Hell is NOT a desirable destination that'd be just what it's supposed to be. Yep. My reasonin's okay. I will check with some religious folks before proceeding. I do confess that there's some serious money involved.

13

TRIP WILEY, M.D.

Hello again. I am Eustice Seeney's friend, physician, and confederate I guess, in this cosmic game of checkers. Chess would be too much for Seeney to finesse, but he's been through plenty. A little background: Through a series of events Seeney died three times. He went to Hell twice, and finally got into Heaven.

Were these events bullshit? Nobody knows for sure. I've served largely as Eustice's foil, and medical provider throughout his journeys. I also kept a log of these events and published them. So there it is look no further. I am motivated by greed, and the excitement of the cosmic gamble that Seeney has been singled out to participate in, and by virtue thereof, I get a piece of.

I am—to an extent—obligated to Seeney, because he bailed me out of some rough situations. Including but not limited to: losing my medical license in the US, and getting it back.

Thanks to Seeney that was restored, and I assisted the man in his lawsuit(s) against the hospitals responsible for his untimely demise, and premature harvesting for organs. Eustice generously afforded me a comfortable sum from his malpractice settlement(s), and I remain indebted to him. So that's where I figure into this. I currently reside in Reno, Nevada, where I work part time for a decrepit general practitioner. As well as an Elvis Impersonator between the ups and downs of my true calling: professional gambling and whoring around. Many years ago, I met, dated, and ultimately married Eustice's niece. We have since divorced. She resides in Australia, and haven't spoken in over a decade. Eustice rarely if ever mentions the brief relation, other than occasionally referring to me as "kin." Which in Eustice's way of thinking must supersede US, state, and international laws.

I haven't had much communication with Eustice since the last time he had an accident, which was really more of an incident. What a scene. Listen up:

That was his third death, and I was beneficiary of his life insurance—the whole "kin" thing"—I mentioned. I truly thought he died for good this third time, even though they couldn't find his body. The authorities called it just that: Death by airboat. He'd had an accident on the swamp "his stompin' grounds." At the time of his death I was working with him saving souls, a calling he had, stemming from his previous experience of going to Hell.

There were some oddballs here and there insisting they were damned, and I helped him out.

It was a temporary situation. I didn't plan on staying long, I wanted to be back in Nevada. Before I got a chance to split he croaked. This time for good, or so I thought. Out of my own guilt, greed, and the money assured me from a life insurance policy, I stuck around to run the: "The Soul Salvation Center," in Florida. An extremely unprofitable enterprise, and thankless treachery that turned out to be. For Eustice, at least a link in a chain that got him into Heaven. I know it's a ridiculous tale, but there's a book about Eustice's trip to Heaven called "Forheavenstake." All that life insurance money had to be repaid when he came back to life. Actually no one knew for sure if he even died because they found his unconscious body. The insurance company thought he was up to some funky shit. I had investigators up the ying, and he had to cover his ass due to the potential charges looming: that he'd faked his death for the insurance money. He spent a ton of loot. Most of the cash he'd gotten from malpractice suits. He set up the "Soul Salvation Center," a real winner—yeah right—that went bust. After the bankruptcy and repayment of funds he moved out to live on the swamp, and I headed west. Its been a year or so since I last heard from him. Personally I think he was resolved, knowing there was an afterlife, and resigned himself to living out his years on familiar ground surrounded by nature. Hey Seeney being Seeney, he had his way.

ME AND MR. MEPHISTOPHELES

I kept in touch on holidays and such, but lately the correspondence increased. Eustice explained that he's got a meeting with Satan, and wants me to help entertain, care for, and make Satan's visit on earth palatable, so he can make Hell more Hellish. Eustice assures me that this will be merely a sightseeing tour for Mr. Mephistopheles, and no foul deeds, crimes or misdemeanors will be involved. Furthermore, the all-expense trip to Florida and healthy stipend should keep me in Elvis sequined suits for a decade. The sum paid by Satan was staggering. In fact, the funds were deposited in a numbered account on Grand Cayman, no strings attached. All he needs is help being Satan's guide, and some medical services. I wasn't exactly in the winner's circle, and the amount of money involved—Marone! My response: Deal me the fuck in.

14

FROM EUSTICE TO SATAN.

Dear Mr. Mephistopheles,

I think you will be pleased to know that no matter what body you settle on for your visit to the mortal world, the best private doctor will be at your disposal. He will treat that flesh you'll be wearin' right fine. Just don't be a douchebag to the fella. That's all squared away on my part, now alls you got to do is find a body nobody will miss.

I am enclosing a list of bodies that you should try to avoid borrowing. As they will not do much other than get you hunted down, put in jail, or put in a mental hospital. Go for something in a medium size without too much muscle, not too fat and not too thin. Yeah, make it thinner so you don't have to bother with too much eatin' of earth food, while you're here. In case you haven't heard, food on earth lately has been real crummy. Processed stuff, too much sugar, blah blah blah. Try to find somebody that doesn't need too much exercise either, on account that's real exhausting shit.

ME AND MR. MEPHISTOPHELES

If you end up with an ordinary body in it's fourth or fifth decade you'll blend right in, and be a generation away from fads and trendy clothes, so's you can save some of your Satanic dollars on threads. Like I said, there'll be a doc here to take care of the usual aches and pains, and stuff that goes crummy. Smart move not choosing a female body on account I'd have to look at your tits. It's a human thing that I'll explain when you get here. Oh yeah, what kind of beer do you drink?

You're friend and host,

Eustice Seeney

* * *

NOTE FROM SATAN

Dear Eustice,

Alas, your hospitality is most appreciated. Of course for what you are being paid no thank you is in order.

Your Satanic Majesty

* * *

DEAR SATAN,

I am writing you today because I have a idea for you that might make Hell more Hellish. You might want to consider this: Having an angry female chamber that looks like a restaurant is a swell idea to the netherworld.
As you know, women think different from fellas, especially with respect to money. They are not such good experts at balancing their checkbooks.

I got a letter from my good ole pal Eddy, he's a real expert on womanology. He knows a whole lot about this, on account he done been divorced a few times, and is always bitchin'. He only dates hookers these days, but I got to talkin' to him and he said he'd send me a note about this.

* * *

15

BROADS A SYNOPSIS

Truly one of the most unpredictably predictable ho's I've ever known. Like most bitches, when it comes down to money, there's HER money, and THE money. HER money is in that special secret pocket, that's HER special ten, twenty bucks. The amount is irrelevant, but universal chick shit. "MY money," is the nickel and dime shit. As if the serious coin that pays the bills doesn't count. Balance a bank account? Sure. That's the shit of science fiction. You KNOW that movie's gonna be rank, when the mathematician's a chick. Yeah, right. Ain't no suspending disbelief there. Like watching a pack of ho's at lunch, sipping their wine, eating this or that. Waiter brings the check and all four ho's go apeshit deciphering how much they owe. An extra twenty cents in chick money? Hell no. You can get your friggin' eyes scratched out. I think there's this overall lack of perception in the big picture, that broads just don't get. Or if they do it's selective to particular situations, when it suits them.

You see, chicks can't answer a direct question. It's impossible. They answer questions with a reminder of something so removed from the conversation that you're thrown off entirely. What the fuck does that have to do with here, now? Of course there's never an answer, that's too touchy. They jump. The jump is they say: I'm having a heart attack, I'm moving out, go ahead take all the [fill in the blank]. Speaking chick is a difficult language. That's why I've come up with this Rosetta Stone language thing to teach guys how to understand chick. Personally I don't really get most of the dialects, but if you go back and look at the cave paintings the chick shit is fucking outrageously undecipherable.

Eddy

* * *

Dear Mr. Mephistopheles,

Having to watch Sex in the City all day at full volume, is more painful than being water-boarded, or so they say. There's plenty of stuff to drive somebody crazy, but I heard homeos was immune to that. That note from Eddy looked pretty right. On account I had me a wife once that ran off with a colored fella when I was in a coma. Collsarn woman took all my velvet Jesus paintings from the trailer, and my lucky coin collection. I reckon those coins weren't so lucky. Well I have to go now. I have been doin' my research for your arrival, and we are almost all set. Please dress accordingly.

Eustice

* * *

16

SATAN: NOTE TO SELF

I certainly hope that some of the rubbish Seeney is providing will be helpful. My concerns are that an automated Hades will be a disaster for all the cosmos. Balderdash to the notion. A mechanized hereafter of damnable quality will remotely accommodate those souls passing through Hell's gates. To these ends, I am preparing myself for an earthly existence, in the event that I am banished from my own domain.

I will implement a "Ladies Eternal Chamber," before leaving. Yes. That might be a start.

I must ready myself for my journey.

6 6 6

17

EUSTICE'S DIARY

Since Ole Mr. Mephistopheles is comin' to town, I thought I'd round up some of the nastiest folks I ever crossed paths with. These are folks who ought be in Hell just on principle alone. I don't reckon goin' out in public with Satan is a might good idea. I know, I know, a lot of folks think incorrectly that Satan is the angel of death. Well that ain't correct. The AOD is a completely separate department, and there's a plenty of them. Sure Satan sits at the board meetings, but he can't make people just get dead. Nope, that's not his department. He can put things in front of them that are bad for 'em, but that's not the same as flat out wompin' someone to death. In fact, the new Rules of Damnation are part of the Overall Scheme of Things, which sort of separates this stuff. Oh yeah, they done modernized. I keep up with this stuff, because your man Eustice is on top of what's in the Grand Plan. I ain't right sure's there is one, but what the hey, right?

* * *

FROM THE DESK OF SATAN:

Ah, so many fresh ideas to "humanize" Hell. I cannot wait to implement some new misery here. Perhaps the outsourcing of some of the damned can be curtailed. I will continue bullshitting Seeney to extract as much data necessary. Seeney must have the long theorized "idiot gene," which The Council of Evil has often discussed. Perhaps a sampling of Eustice's DNA might reveal it's location, and we can begin breeding morons. This would be helpful because at some point Eustice became aware of Hell's secrets, and this is a gene we must mutate. Hell has no margin for error, and the likes of this simpleton escaping cannot occur again. I shall contact our human laboratories to isolate this, and rid Hades for all time of potential threats to my eminence of the underworld. Bah, no one escapes Hell unless I say so. Ah, a letter has arrived from Seeney, let's see what this is about . . .

* * *

Dear Mister Mephistopheles,

I have been carefully considering things that might be useful for the new Hades. Right now in the US of A is a whole bunch of stuff that should be right nice to make people want to throw up all day, and regret being there.

ME AND MR. MEPHISTOPHELES

Make people watch twenty four hour news. Maybe for the gals, on account making the fellas watch reruns of chick shows is crummy. Gals not only hate the news channels, they go nuts when it's on all day.

Eustice

* * *

Part 2

SATAN'S LOG: EARTH DATE #1

I arrived in Cleveland at 10 a.m. Tuesday, in February. I have been in this place for thirty-seconds and already miss Hell.

Per the directions from The Powers That Be, I can only utilize a human whose life is at its expiration date. The cusp of death, so to speak. I made my preferences clear as to age and gender, this was it. Egads. How revolting. I found a homeless, human male body, age approximately 45, give or take ten years. This remarkably malnourished specimen is foul smelling, even by Hell standards, and has an odd craving for Sterno, or some alcohol based product. I feel the sandpaper texture of tissue on my face, and an urge to urinate. I have matted hair on my head, and my vision is adequate, as well as my hearing. This is a body that no human will miss. I am wearing jeans, a few layers of clothing, some sort of foot covering—shoes —that are remarkably uncomfortable.

ME AND MR. MEPHISTOPHELES

Hmm . . .my feet have not taken human form yet, and the webbing between my toes is irritating. Make note to self to have this tended to. Painful feet may be useful in the new Hades. There is a wallet, driver's license, and two US dollars. There is a pack of cigarettes.

This could be fun. Certainly I can fix this vessel up and get on with being human, albeit only briefly. I am still trying to accustom myself to the constraints of physicality. There are some odd sensations that seem to travel along pathways and burst in the skull casing like a supernova, or meteorologic event. Starbursts and waterfalls? Not exactly. More like what humans would call agony and crippling pain. I will need to refurbish this heap prior to getting along with things. The discomfort the body is experiencing slows it down far too much. These things called feet? Egads they ache. Make note to include pain in soles of human feet. A postmortem experience. Will need to research possibilities.

I am in an alley under gray skies, and am not attired for the climate. I will, according to the PTB, have use to my Satanic cosmic debit card and do some shopping before I begin my journey. To resolve the issues needing adjustment. Among them, that nuisance Seeney.

6 6 6

18

Hey it's me Eustice. I ain't heard back from Ole Mister Mephistopheles for a spell, and got to wonderin' if I'm bein' played. I done rapped with my pals, got letters and stuff, and that devil of a Devil ain't writ back. I reckon he can go fuck himself. After all I got stuff to do. Who's got the time to piss away waitin' on some bull-pucky from Hell? I know, it sounds crazy as a gum-ball machine that spits out gold for a quarter. I'm just gonna do my thing, and if Satan shows up he shows up. When or if he does, that ole Devil's gonna be in for a real surprise. I know how sneaky that critter is, and figure if I can catch him— you know like a bull gator or some other beast—and hornswoggle him into a cage, I can score big in The overall scheme of things.

I got me a plan. Yep. I am gonna consult with some folks and set me up a Devil Trap, and ransom Satan off. I gotta reckon there's a buck to be turned on that maneuver, right? Yeah, you know what I mean.

ME AND MR. MEPHISTOPHELES

I figure the shit that pisses off Satan the most and neutralizes his demoniacal, ectoplasmic, zeotropic powers over people: is that temptation that he waves in front of them. If I can catch him in human form and dope him up but good he ain't gonna be nothin' but some other rummy on the street.

* * *

SATAN'S LOG EARTH DATE #1.5

I managed to adorn myself with some of humankind's finest attire, a haircut, manicure, and will be visiting the Cleveland Clinic to tune up this lump of flesh. This absurd rotting bag of chemicals, that shits, pisses, and is imbued with remarkably stunning aches, pains, longings, and desires. How useful to actually experience some of man's own attributes. Hopefully these can be remedied post-haste.

Hell knows what else is in store for me in this miserable populace before heading toward Florida, the most wretched part of the so-called Free World. Final destination prior to departure. Heaven's Waiting Room? Ha. Many of Hades arrivals suggest: Florida is a prime example of a new balmier vision of Hades.

Today I began feeling some odd sensations in my new body. They seem to come in waves when I see the female version of human. I do not get this sensation when I see others with the same, or similar body styles. The pyunal member, which I have manipulated from Hell to tempt humans for eons, is now attached above my new balls.

I believe that upon viewing the chest appendages, those spheroid chest mounds, I shall experience what humans refer to as "boners." This will be interesting, learning how to wield this piece of flesh.

666

19

THE SATAN TRAP

Eustice Goes to the Hardware Store

Seeney, in this unusual circumstance began preparation for the tentative arrival of Satan, and began constructing the Satan Trap.

I called Doc Wiley, who'd already agreed to come on down and we'd set things up. He and Eddy M, another doctor, figured that there was more money in fuckin' with this shit than in the doctorin' racket. They was waitin' for me in the parkin' lot.

"Hey Eustice," Wiley said, "you know Eddy, right?"

"I talked to him a few times, but we ain't never met." Eustice looks over at the other gent and says: "Hellfire, I know you. I met you over at the last hospital I sued. You're one of the docs that got fired."

"Yeah, that's right," Eddy said merrily. "I hated those fuckers. Wiley says you got a fat score kidnapping Satan, and I'm good for a cut on that deal."

"Sure Eddy, but you gotta have pure intentions."

"Fuck that shit. I wanna make some bank, is that pure enough? I already sent you a 'How to fuck someone up letter', figure that'd buy me a seat at this poker game."

"Eustice," Wiley interrupted. "Eddy is a bit raw. He just got out of prison."

"Prison! Hellfire. What in tarnation'd you do Eddy? Kill somebody?"

"Tried too."

"Shee-yatt. You're a crazy man. I don't know, maybe Satan already got dibs on you."

"That's the point isn't it Eustice, if you're gonna build a trap, you need some bait. Eddy over there is flawed."

"Who the fuck're you calling flawed Wiley? I'll fucking rip your lungs out and shit down your neck."

"Simmer down now fellas, simmer down. We gotta make us a Demon trap." Eustice stressed.

"You hear that Eddy?"

"Yeah, yeah. I'm cool with that."

The three of them went into the Zeus Hardware Emporium in Golden Springs, Florida that day. What they left with cost nine thousand seven hundred and twenty dollars and sixty seven cents.

"Eustice, do you know if Satan's going to be taking a male or female body?" Wiley asked.

"Why'd he wanna be a chick, man?" Eddy asked.

"Eddy, he was asking me." Eustice said.

"Doc, I don't right know. But he's probably gonna get a body he can get the most use out of?"

"Yeah maybe he'll be a hot looking ho." Eddy said.

"Nah, I reckon he'd be a dude so's he can beat up people and shit. That's more like the Devil I know." Eustice said.

Wiley said: "Eustice may be right, a woman would be more upkeep."

"Shit Wiley, you sound like more of a misogynist than me. Broads can get away with more shit. That'd be my guess." Eddy replied.

"No, no, no. You gotta figure if Satan's gonna take a body its gotta have some oomph to it. He'll be able to beat the shit outta people fuckin' with him, and not have to fuck around with that period shit. Tits and all can get in the way of that." Eustice said.

"Tell that to the fuckin' feminist ho's." Eddy scrunched up his mouth, shook his head, laughed mirthlessly, and spit out: "Bitches, fuckin' bitches, man."

"Eddy," Wiley said, "It's no wonder you've had five wives, you got zero sensitivity."

"Would you two shut the Hell up, blah blah blah. He's gonna be a dude." Eustice said.

"Yeah, what if he gets a homo body, huh?" Eddy chimed in.

"That'd be pretty funny." Wiley said.

"Yeah he'd be all politically correct, or, we'd have to be all politically correct. A homo Satan. Nah. Nobody'd buy it. Who the fuck would choose to be a homo? Nah, I may not be politically correct, but only an idiot would choose a homo frame, interior, and sound system," Eddy said.

"Ya'all talkin' 'bout bodies like cars." Eustice added.

"Same shit," Eddy said.

"Eddy's lost his license, been sued a dozen times, and spent time in lockup."

"Then it's settled," Wiley said. "Satan's going to be a dude, who's probably going to be vulnerable as such."

"Yep. That's what I reckon too," Eustice nodded.

* * *

SATAN'S LOG EARTH DATE #2

I am becoming accustomed to this human form. Yesterday I visited a "tit bar," where I experienced continuous boners. One of the nude females noticed, and in exchange for earth dollars gave me instruction on its use. This was enjoyable, and I have taken to human breasts as a fine way to pass earth time. I am uncertain if all females will allow me to examine their breasts in exchange for money. I will look into this at a later time. Today I must visit the maintenance of human bodies at the Clinic as previously noted.

666

NOTE :DOCTOR'S EXAMINATION AND REPAIR.

I presented to the facility primarily because the ramshackle body I borrowed is: undoubtedly poorly fueled, suffers with some earthly malady, and can use some medications or preparations. I have more than adequate funds, infinite earthly resources, and will be "tuned up" by the highest quality care—by human standards—earth has to offer. I am uncertain as to the proper fuel to put in this wreck of a body. I have no idea what the correct admixture of substances this bag of protoplasm requires. I suspect it sensible to get professional inspection, especially if I am going to be using it for any length of time. The Powers that Be gave me 7 Days. Imagine that. The same amount of time the alleged creator of the "Heavens and the Earth," took to create mankind. Bah, I say. There was nothing in those "Holy Books" describing my domain. Bah. Nonetheless, I must comply, or by contract I will be dispatched posthaste, to some outpost in another solar system. Perhaps I can wrap this up sooner.

NOTE TO MINIONS: Big Mac is excellent and tempting, as are Wise potato chips. The alcoholic beverages this body seems to crave taste horrible, and seem to dull the abilities of its use. Will be discussing this with medical provider.

6 6 6

20

SATAN AT THE CLINIC

I did some preliminary research regarding the finest body shops on earth at the geographic location I would be landing. A regal temple of human health I must say. Reminiscent somewhat of the Egyptian Pyramids. To bad they didn't build them. Aliens. Ha. Maybe Rome's Colosseum? At least that was a human effort. Those animals would pit one human against another for sport, idiots. Many among them were inconsolable. They would age and die. More intent on bringing about suffering. Ah, those were the days. When an eternity in Hell was indeed Hellish. Nothing on earth could compare to being damned for all time. At least humans could offer each other a quick and painless death before I got them. Or worse if they were pure, whatever that is, they went to the bright white light, Heaven. Ha. What a joke that was. Blah blah blah, as Seeney would say. NOTE TO SELF: Do not quote Eustice Seeney.

A lovely facility indeed. Several stories in height, architecturally akin to some of the finest places of worship made by humans. Guarded too, with armed sentinels. I simply waved my hand and walked past the lobby guards without more than a smile, or a "Hello sir welcome to the clinic." I still had some degree of mind control over these imbecile humans.

The doctor I was to see was acclaimed the finest of them all. His office was on the fourth floor. Its waiting room adorned with art—copies of the original—some masters whose soul I took in exchange for the talent they may have had. Also an aquarium—lovely they are—sea creatures in a bowl, above earth level, miles and miles away from their home. For reasons known only to The Powers That Be, sea dwellers did not cede to my telepathic influence, and seemed to congeal as if in unison to show me disrespect. When my minions would visit, schools of fish would form a "V" shape and menacing appearance. No, the sea was no friend of Hades. Must have been that run in with Ulysses, and mishap in my domain. Prick managed to escape MY turf. Fuck you fish. I flicked a finger at the glass, just as the doctor's secretary slid the glass pane to call a patient in. I waved my hand and she stopped mid-sentence. Replacing my name for one of the many patients awaiting a visit with the esteemed physician. Ha. Satan comes first. I wanted to send a lightning bolt down on that waiting room and all the sick people, but this crummy body did have its limitations. So I allowed another female, a nurse, judging by her costume, to escort me to a room.

ME AND MR. MEPHISTOPHELES

The examination room was laid out with the basics: table, sink, exam stool, X-ray view light, and cabinets. A fortyish well groomed man—I appeared—in a gown with an open back, studying the neon lights, exam lamp, and prints of off-the-rack artwork adorning the walls. There is a chart of the human musculoskeletal system, another of the digestive system, and a "no smoking" sign. I lit up a cigarette, something learned at the tit bar earlier. The door burst open almost immediately after the first pull.

"What are you doing?" A woman with some papers in her hand opened the door, snatched the cigarette, and rushed to the room's sink. Turning on the faucet she put her face within inches of the Devil—unaware of who I am after all, The Prince of Darkness. She began scolding me. "No smoking or you will be removed from this facility."

"Excuse me?" Satan says, staring at this female specimen. A bit confused: She IS female, but her hair is cut short, her features gray and sagging, her voice deep, like she is speaking from the bottom of one of Hell's pits. Her tone is harsh, authoritative. If she has tits, he doesn't even want to look at them. "Madame, I don't think you are. . . ." he shut up quickly before finishing: "Aware that I can lay your soul to waste." Rather politely said: "Sorry won't happen again."

"It better not Mr. Sifer," she had her fists balled up on wide hips. "Lewis Sifer, I have your number don't try that again."

This must be the bull dyke version of human body style. What would that nincompoop Seeney say: Bleah. Yes, that's good. Bleah.

"Doctor will be in momentarily." She pivoted and walked out of the room like some horrid creature.

SATAN'S NOTE TO MINIONS: Stock Hell with several thousand of these.

6 6 6

"Hello I'm Dr. Seigenstien, how are we today?"

Satan looked over his shoulder, then back at the short, balding, bespectacled man in a white coat, that hung below his knees. "We?"

"Yes, you and I."

"Jew?"

"Excuse me, Mr. Sifer?"

"Oh dear. Where I come from there are few of the Mosaic Faith."

"Where might that be?" The doctor asked.

"South, I am from the Deep Deep South," Satan responded.

"What brings you here today?"

Shit I have to tell this Hebrew everything about myself, and this bullshit rummy body I've borrowed. Damn this fucker to Hell, but I can't because Jews have their own fucking Hell. Shit shit shit.

NOTE TO MINIONS: I must have pissed off this human Hebrew. He stuck his fingers in every orifice. Then had some cherubic fumbling Negro stick needles in me to remove blood, and sent me to a chamber to scan my borrowed body.

6 6 6

"Mr. Sifer. Lewis, do you mind if I call you Lewis?"

"No, not at all."

"Good Lewis, please put your clothes on. My nurse will escort you to my consultation room, so we can go over your test results. I have to make a few calls, give me a few minutes."

"A few minutes?" Satan said.

"We pride ourselves on efficiency." The doctor beamed, and notched his chin toward his embroidered name in blue thread on his coat. "This is the top medical center in the world. I won't be long."

"I know doctor, that is what they say."

"I don't want you to take this the wrong way Lewis, but I think it best you remain here until we've gone over your case."

"I believe that I can be the judge of that." Satan said.

"Oh, you're a doctor I suppose." The man in the white coat shook his head. "I've found some rather unusual things we need to go over."

"I know what I need." Satan said.

"Really, what did you need me for?"

"Confirmation and some other little things. Don't worry. If you're smart, smart as all those acronyms behind your name, you're going to forget all about me after I leave."

"We'll see about that Mr. Sifer. I can't do that."

"Really doctor. I think we should step into your consultation room now." Lewis held out his hand, palm facing the doctor and pushed him toward his private office down the hall.

Dr. Seigenstien felt a force like an opposing pole of a magnet against his chest and stumbled backwards. "What are you doing?"

"Just move it."

"You're barely living!" The doctor said.

"Silence." Satan said.

"Who are you?"

"Just do as I say. Open the door and sit down. I need some things."

The doctor's back was against a door with his name on it followed by his title. He fumbled for the doorknob and twisted it, as he maintained eye contact with Sifer. "Are you threatening me?" He fell backward. Righted himself, and opened his mouth.

"Silence." Lewis Sifer held up his hand.

They were in a dimly lighted room with walls of books, and a large desk cluttered with papers. There was a big leather chair on one side, with a wall of diplomas behind it. Two client chairs faced the wall. Lewis Sifer sat down and said without preamble: "I know this body is—for all practical medical purposes—barely living. Your findings are accurate. It's riddled with cancer, heart disease, and years of Sterno consumption, having destroyed its thought processes. But I assure you doctor, that is irrelevant. I have little use for this body, merely to keep it running until I am finished with it."

"What? What are you talking about—you're practically dead—I can't do anything for you."

"But you will. I need medications and your silence."

"I can't do that." The doctor said.

"You can and you will."

"Or . . ."

"I will strike you down now." A letter opener flew across the desk into Satan's hand.

"Telekinesis? No, this can't be happening ."

"This goes into your left eye doctor. Five seconds to comply . . ."

"I can't," the doctor gripped the arms of his chair.

"You can and you will." Satan said.

"But you're nearly de, dead." The doctor said.

"The astute physician. Just do as I say and life will go on." Sifer added.

"If I don't?" The doctor replied.

"One wrong word to anyone after you're finished and you'll find out."

666

21

EUSTICE AND CREW

The telephone rang at Eustice's place. It was Trip Wiley, MD.

"Hey Doc," Eustice said. "No I ain't too busy. Just busy enough." Seeney had taken to sipping slow beers and munching Cheetos, while catching up on the day's events in front of his TV set. He was awaiting a choice opportunity: to challenge Satan to a cosmic chess game. Of course checkers would have been simpler. Seeney knew that Mephistopheles would be armed with thousands of years of wisdom, the most cantankerous of trickery, and pack more wallop than a thousand bull gators collectively en route to shit out the crappy Sterno swilling wino they mistakenly consumed.

"Eustice," Wiley said. "I think we can ensnare the Devil with a little help from the women in our lives, and some real doozies."

"Do tell, Doc?" Eustice snapped open another beer and took a sip.

"Can you call some of your neighbors Eustice?"

"I don't right know. I reckon if I offered `em free booze or food, maybe they'd see fit to drop by. They're all hermits, kinda like me. They keep to themselves, not fans of strangers. Some even maybe hidin out from one thing or another. Be tough? What you got in mind?"

"I think we need a crowd, a noisy one. Maybe make it look like we're making a dirty movie. That shit would drive anyone mad. I think we need to throw a bogus cast party. I know just who to call," Trip said. "An open house for the Devil. Give him a taste of earth's finest. I think I can get Eddy to go along. Botox injections and I'll offer free cosmetic surgery."

"Doc, you ain't no plastic surgeon." Eustice said.

"So what? Eddy was until they pulled his license, and I can wing anything. I can rustle up plenty of gals to keep Satan spinning in circles as they fawn all over him. That's when we spring our trap!"

"What trap, doc?"

"I'll tell you in person. Go on and call around. I know you're friends with a pimp in Palm Beach. Round up the skankiest broads you can Eustice. We're talking Jerry Springer's rejects. Satan wants to improve Hell? We'll give it to him. He won't come back to earth for eons if we work this right. You dig?"

"I'm on it, but I'm gonna need your help." Eustice crumpled up his cheese puff bag, and set out on his recon mission. The trailer park and surrounding shopping plaza would be filled with gals, ripe, ready, and set to meet a couple of doctors for free consultations. There was going be a regular welcome wagon for Satan, once that old devil finally blows into town.

"I'm with you, but . . ."

"I'll be expectin' you, Doc." Eustice hung up.

* * *

22

SATAN GETS A BAD REVIEW

One hour seventeen minutes and thirty-seconds later, Lewis Sifer, stood on the sidewalk in front of the medical center. He had vials of pills in the side pocket of his suit coat. They were waiting for him at the clinics pharmacy. The man was well aware of electronic prescribing, and knew very well what medicines were being prescribed. He also knew how to hack into the electronic message from that Hebrew physicians office to the pharmacy. Bing, bang, boom. The druggist didn't even flinch at the enormous quantities of potent pain medicines, stimulants, and other odds and ends Satan deemed suitable for this rent-a-wreck, Ha. Make that steal-a-wreck of rotting flesh he was occupying. Like some orbital on an atom about to be imploded upon. Ha.

Lewis Sifer stared at a slip of paper, instructions and orders for scans. He crumpled it up and threw it into the right lane of traffic.

It struck the windshield of Elmer Fuddish's recently washed, waxed, and detailed 2004, F-150 pickup truck.

"Motherfucker!" The man took off his beige—almost white—brand spanking new Stetson hat, and laid it gently on the bench seat, just before the full impact of chemical pathways kicked in. It took seconds for his amygdala, hypothalamus, pituitary, and adrenals to kick into full "fight or flight" fury. Boom, he wasn't gonna fly!

In a furious burst of adrenaline, he slammed his steel toed, waterproof, work boot foot on the brake pedal. Raising his flannel shirt sleeved arms and balled up fists he shouted "I'm gonna kick your ass Mr. Fancy Pants." He pounded his chest once and said: "Right now asshole, put `em up."

His rant drew a crowd, a small one at that. This human race can be so predictable. "Oh please," Lewis said softly, patting his pill pocket."

"Who the fuck you thing you are asshole?" He raised his voice by several decibels cursing at the dapper man in the dark blue Brioni suit. Lewis stood tapping a Gucci shoe, and shaking his head. Elmer's nose was two centimeters from that of the Prince of Darkness's borrowed beak.

Within seconds the day strollers gathered. Some of them stopped in their tracks while others scattered, or joined the circle forming around the two men.

One of the passerby folks would later recall, that the well dressed man spoke in a curt resonating tone, that sounded like the words could slice through steel. They didn't however, slice through anything but a tense atmosphere.

His words carried mellifluously: "You will give me your vehicle."

With those words, the six foot two Elmer Fuddish did so.

"Please please take this," Elmer held out his palm. "What's mine is yours." At that he was reduced to a sniveling, weeping man on his knees, begging for the man in the suit to take everything he had. His pockets were turned inside out, tears streamed down his cheeks.

An onlooker, a large man of African descent, grabbed Elmer above his left elbow and helped him to his feet. Then shoved him up against a wall and slapped his cheek. "Snap out of it, Mon."

The man was stunned at first by the accent. Jamaican jigaboo? What the Hell was this? It was as if he hadn't just given his truck away to the Devil.

"What're you doin' ya big . . ." The truck driver said.

The black man socked him hard just below the ribs, knocking the air out of his lungs, and watched him slide down the clinics marble wall. "You'll be fine," he said making sure he hadn't harmed him before he stepped away.

He stood face-to-face with the dapper dressed, gray skinned man. The two men locked eyes. For a fraction of a second the breathless, bitch slapped, shaken, albeit mindful Elmer, would recall the Negro being at least several feet taller than him.

"Who do you think you are?" The black man spoke.

"You don't want to know." Lewis said.

"I wouldn't bet on it," the black man said, patting him gently on the shoulder. "No, I would not be making that bet at all."

"Piss off darky." Lewis turned his face from the man, patted his side pocket, and began walking slowly toward the 2004, F-150 pickup truck. The crowd parted like stalks of corn in the path of an oncoming combine. Ha. Mr. Fuddish's hat fit just right. Lewis looked at himself in the truck's rearview mirror, adjusted the cowboy hat, and smiled. He marveled that despite the ashen face, the decaying sack of flesh he'd borrowed at least had a nice set of pearly white false teeth. Probably from some dental school trainee, he thought. As they were grossly enormous. In fact, they looked like dice cubes. The Devil drummed his wrinkled fingers on them, and gunned the engine. This was going to be fun.

6 6 6

23

MEDICAL ERRORS?

Dr. Seigenstien looked at the papers on his desk, and for the life of him couldn't find anything in writing from his patient, Lewis Sifer. Where the Hell was it? He had to make this right. The pharmacist called, and was on hold. They had already filled his prescriptions, and the pharmacist claimed that she spoke with him. "I never had a word with you about Mr. Sifer," he said. The doctor had no such dialogue and knew it. What the Hell was this about?

"I called you immediately when Mr. Sifer came for his meds," Amina Toulinin PharmD said, in a tone reserved for pill counting, not quite authoritarian. "But I WILL turn your ass over to the DEA in a heartbeat. You authorized all of it. You are denying this?"

"No. No I'm not denying anything. I just need to find the paperwork," Seigenstien said.

"I certainly hope so doctor. I have my duties as you have yours."

"Of course." Dr. S. knew that bitch would jump at the chance to rat his ass out for anything. Argh. He'd been duped and he knew it. That fucking pharmacist has had it out for me for years. Dammit!

"He should be back here soon," Dr. Seigenstien said, a huge rush of anxiety in his voice. "He's got a scan scheduled."

"I hope so for your sake, doctor. Cocaine, morphine, amphetamines, and enough refills to cross the Eastern Seaboard."

"Is that all?" Dr. S. heard a tap on his door.

The pharmacist hung up just as his nurse entered the consultation room. "I think you better take a look at this," she said.

"What?"

"The aquarium," she said. "Come and see."

"I've got enough on my plate, just tell me?"

"The fish are . . ."

"What?" He asked.

She sat down in one of the exam room chairs in front of his desk. "Dead, and that man Sifer? He left this for you."

Dr. S picked up the slip of paper, and leaned back in his plush chair. It let out a whoosh that sounded more like a fart to the woman across from him.

The doctor made a series of phone calls. Logged on to his bank and brokerage accounts, as well as, the state license verification page. He had been deleted.

"Shit," he said. That prick wasn't kidding.

"Cancel my appointments."

* * *

24

OFF TO MEPHIS

SATAN: NOTE TO SELF:

Those imbeciles. I cannot wait until I meet them. Having this piece of trash body is cumbersome, but it certainly has not slowed down my powers. Ha. I truly must confess the limitations of the flesh. I have constant cravings for drugs, alcohol, and prostitutes. I have become fond of the female breasts, and the smell of a woman's crotch. Make note: for the improved Hades to stock up on untouchable tits which cause pain upon palpation. Ha. I am very pleased I did not borrow a homosexual body. Maybe next time. Hmm, no. Make that a portion in Hades where the homosexuals are damned with serial enemas for eternity with applesauce, and no toilet paper. Further note: Lesbian section of Hades. Research needed. I must make a point of removing the good drugs from Hades, and perhaps paying my minions in narcotics. Yes. Onward toward grander earthly research. Must send note to Seeney.

25

SATAN'S LOG: EARTH DATE 3

The human body can be a most uncomfortable place to inhabit. The sleep function is disturbing in the body I have chosen. It refuses to stop reeling thought processes, despite the time spent on attempting to have them cease. I remained awake at a Night's Inn Motor Lodge for six hours before finally reaching the "sleep state," which was rich with images that I did not recall upon awakening. At the awakening the body had urges to excrete material which was foul smelling, and abundant. The penis ached for nearly thirty minutes before it was drainable. The movement of the body's arms, legs, toes, fingers, and its back, neck, and skull aches. Pain. This is a novel concept that must be experienced to fully appreciate. The medication prescriptions the clinic practitioner provided had been crunchy to chew, but thanks to the large jugs of alcohol readily available at any shop, they were made easy to wash down. It is confusing how humans make a big deal over tiny pills, and a "doctor" must write out a note to obtain them.

The following pill bottles are in my possession: Diazepam, Hydrocodone, Carisoprodol, Temazepam, Metformin, rosuvastatin, and sildenafil, which the doctor told me to take to keep this body functioning. I awoke with trembling fingers that were relieved with a container filled with Vodka. The prostitute I hired last night left after one hour, and refused to take my Hades charge card. Then sent a huge Negro—was all of this world run by Negroes nowadays—to collect money. I had to remove his nastiness, and dispose of his and the prostitute's terrified bodies. They began making pleas for their eternal souls so loud, it drowned out the Andy of Mayberry marathon I was watching on television, while penetrating every orifice with my fleshy wand. Make note to minions: for special gallery of whores in the New Hades blueprint. Since I am not permitted to remove life only render them, Make note: to provide plenty of pain in the afterlife. Scratch that. Since humans will not have body after death. Have minions study new ways to connect physical pain to souls.

6 6 6

26

SATAN ON THE ROAD

I am going to discard the vehicle I borrowed from the dolt I took yesterday. The seats were uncomfortable, and use the pimp's luxurious car. After filling him with terror, he offered to turn the Cadillac Coupe deVille's keys over to me, and signed a slip of paper that he said, was the "pink slip," that indicates I am the car's owner. The music is interesting but irritates my human ears, and evokes an ache in my head. "Bitches and Ho's boom boom boom" over and over. This is music in this era? At least Mozart had some soothing sounds, this shit belongs in Hell. Fortunately there is a Tom Jones disc to play, and asking the pussycat what is new is pleasant for driving. Apparently this skill, driving, as well as the ones used with the prostitute, fucking, came with the disease ridden body. Perhaps a healthier specimen would have made my trip to the corporeal world more enjoyable. But no this is NOT a vacation.I must remind myself, that if I do not find new ways to increase the horror level of Hell, I'll be shit out of a job.

I should find some time to watch a few horror movies. I will let my earth guide take care of that. I do wonder if that nincompoop Seeney will have access to movie theaters in his living area. Hmm. This makes me wonder if he has some other terrifying things to study. I will write him after my drive. It would have been nice to fly, but those airport people—so I have gleaned from watching television news—are very fussy with respect to going through your things. I do not want earth people going through my notes, or the medicines and materials I have collected so far.

According to the clinics doctor, this body will not last as long as ordinary bodies. This has some heart problems, blood pressure problems, and arthritis, and the doctor said it might have cancer. So I best gather what I must as quickly as possible. Maybe I should refrain from stopping off at Graceland?

Hmm. There are cigarettes in the pink motor vehicle called KOOL. The body has an urge to smoke them. Okay. This body seems to have many behaviors programmed into it. There is a rumbling in the gut portion, and the body's mind has images of yellow arches, and the words: Big Mac, fries, chocolate shake. I will leave the expressway I am driving on, and locate an eating establishment. I suspect I will find a room to excrete more brown smelly material.

6 6 6

SATAN'S LOG: MIDDLE OF DAY #4 ADDENDUM

The nourishment for this feeble bag has a variety of tastes. Some evocative of revulsion, others curiously enjoyable (note: this is the word of Satan, do not indicate ANY earthly pleasure). The two all beef patties, special sauce, etc. is indeed a marvelous invention. One of my minions encouraged its developer to pursue. And the fries? As some would say: "To die for." If they only knew. I have consumed six of them today, along with some other delights, and have a need to purge these things. Must sign off to vomit.

6 6 6

27

EUSTICE AT HOME AWAITIN' SATAN

I gotta tell you that havin' Ole Mister Mephistopheles comin' by to hang out is gonna be a real humdinger of a slumber party. I already got Doc Wiley and one of his doctor friends on notice so's to dope him, and show that sucker some real human aches and pains. I know it ain't quite right to treat your guests mean, but this IS the DEVIL collsarn it. And iffen I don't oblige the guy by showin' that Ole Devil that Hell's not all it's cut out to be I'd be a might remissible in my duties as a human, right?

Doc Wiley says we ought have us a real wing ding, and I done started linin' up everybody I could to make a right fine block party for my new buddy. You see I ain't right sure how Satan's gonna take to all this. Hang on somebody's knockin' at the door.

I go peek out the window, and there's this tall, twerpy lookin' fella, in a suit and tie, and Ray Ban Wayfarer shades. Standin' there with some papers.

Damn! That there might be a collsarn process server. Shee-yat. I gotta be real quiet, on account tweren't me, nope. Uh-uh, no way. I didn't do but for nothin', maybe it's a mistake. Hmm. I gotta think on this. There's my ex-wife, I think she's dead though, or married to that colored fella she was gettin' poked by while I was in a coma. That ole bee-yatch didn't know it, but I sure's Hell may've been un-concho, but I know'd she was gettin' snaked right there on my hospital bed! I gotta reckon she found out about all that money I'd got from my lawsuits, and wants a piece of the action. Its been a spell, but that ole gal always was a money hound. She'd be sayin': "Eustice, you lazy good for nothin' bum go out and make some money, blah blah blah."

Then just like that it occurred to me she done upped and died way back when. That's right. I forgot she tripped over the cord of my life support lung pumper on the way to gettin' herself hosed. And in the throes of humpin,' dangled a bare foot into the puddle of pee from the bag that broke, and got herself electrocuted. I don't right remember what happened to the colored guy, but that don't matter, on account that sucker's still bangin' on my door. Hoowee. I best call up the lawyer man and ask if anybody's out suin'. Shh, I gotta be real quiet.

I got the phone in the bathroom, and called the law office. I must've been on hold for two cycles of crummy music. Finally some husky voice lady asks what I want. I whisper to the secretary I wanna talk to the lawyer, and tell her to have him check and see on the clerk of court files if there's anybody, anywhere, comin' after me. I already figured it weren't, on account I aint broke any laws. Or there'd be some cops. Nope. None of that. Collsarn secretary says the lawyer's too busy. Sumbitch is always too busy. I made that basserd plenty of loot from my unlawful medical errors and malpractice suits over the years. He ought pick up the phone lickety-split when I call. But no—too busy for Eustice. Screw that sumbitch. His secretary gets back on the line, I reckon she used the special lawyer computer stuff to do some checkin', and says: "No Mr. Seeney, there are no suits filed, no bench warrants, no one is looking for you. Is that all?"

Click.

Click? What the Hell's that all about? I didn't even get to say too-da-loo, and that filly hangs up on me? There I am standin' in the bathtub with the phone in my hand, listenin' to some geeky guy in a suit in 80 degree weather with papers. That's about when I realized it might be someone workin' for the Devil hisself. Hmm, only Satan can get me all hibbidy jibbidy like this, and that there must be one of his minions. I go on over to the door and since I'm about to be a fine host open up and say: "Howdy."

"Hello Sport," the fella with papers says to me.

"Do I know you?" I say.

He lowered his sunglasses.

Hoowee, it's the collsarn bartender from Hell! I know it for sure on account he ain't got no eyeballs. Nope, he got mirrors in his eye sockets, like he was wearin' mirrored contact lenses. He's got that same piss poor smarmy tone he had when I was in Hell. Pansy sorta fella talks at me like one of them clerks at a fancy hotel in that: "If you have to ask how much it is you can't afford it tone." Fuck that, I say to myself.

"What do you want?" I say. I know he ain't got no business here in the corporeal world, and he can't be outta Hell too long or he'll just turn to dust. Don't ask how I know that, but you gotta suspend disbelief, or watch some vampire movies to do your checkin'.

"These are for you." He holds out some papers like they're dirty diapers filled with poo.

"These from your boss?" I say.

"Just take them Sport."

"They must be a might more important than them letters sendin' you on over from Hades, right?"

He just stands there and starts tappin' his foot like a waiter who ain't been tipped.

Finally he says: "You have to sign for this," and holds out some sorta clipboard.

"Just put your thumbprint on it." He shakes his head like he's talkin' to some dummy, or a kid with that same pretentious air in his voice. "You really are an imbecile, Sport."

"Listen up sonny," I say. "You ain't got no business here, and if you call me 'Sport' one more time I'll take a ball bat and cattywomp you till you're a pile of crumbs." Of course I know he ain't got any real corporeal body, but it's always good to show these minions of Satan who's boss.

"Just take the papers and I'll be on my way . . . Sport." I grab `em, and the fella puts his shades back on, clicks his heels like some Nazi, fairy in the Land of Oz, and just like that, poof! He disappears into thin air. Well it ain't so thin, on account the humidity's real high. Freakin' crumb ought been et by a gator or somethin', give him a what's what here on earth. Dickhead. Glad to see that fucker's gone.

I go back inside and see it's a letter from Satan's legal department. It has a seal of sorts on it with a spooky design. It looks all fancy and ancient like it came from Dracula's castle and all. I get to readin' it and know I can't show it to my earth lawyer. Hoowee, it's a nondisclosure agreement that says I can't tell nobody about Satan comin' to learn about fixin' Hades in the event that he gets fired. Right then I actually get to thinkin' Ole Mister Mephistopheles is really on the verge of gettin' fired. Well, I got my work cut out. Why? Well that old sayin' "The Devil you know is better than the one you don't," applies here. If Satan, the one I tangled with is replaced, Hell just might be one big ole computerized mess. Hell, it might be run by robot aliens.

* * *

SATAN'S LOG EARTH DATE #5

I awoke this morning at a motel off the highway on my way to Eustice Seeney's place. I paid for the room via Hades Express Card, and ordered out pizza and another prostitute to explore my many human fetishes. The crappy body I am using is truly a broken down wreck. I would have preferred a better model or edition, but circumstances prevailed, and this had to do. Piece of shit body. After extensive fucking and pizza eating this body just gave out. I discovered—thanks to the prostitute—how to use toilet paper, the meaning of blowjobs, and bathing. What the body can do when it is fueled with the right combination of drugs, alcohol, and other forms of stimulation. I would like to have known some of the basic details on body care before leaving Hades, but will make do. Fell into this sleep thing and had brain function. This body is a real piece of shit. The experiences are out-and-out horrid. To imagine that Hell is eternal horror. Waking up in a body like this? Bad Heavens! This is abhorrent. I can barely sleep. The fluid that comes out of this thing all night long, and the feces? The foul smelling mess, and that is just the start of it. No wonder so many humans kill themselves. I can barely clench the fingers to make a fist, so I can beat some other human. One of my favorite damnable ploys, getting humans to fight. The Powers That Be certainly designed this lump of flesh filled with chemicals as a test, that much is certain. I cannot wait to leave this heap of chemicals. Thank Hades I got those medications for this piece of junk. I must take them too. One to make my head stop reverberating, another so it lasts through the week. That imbecile body repairman, the "doctor," warned me I was doomed. Ha. Me doomed? If that fool only knew I was the Prince of Darkness himself. Fortunately I can fuel this heap with booze. I can drink and drink and take the lovely dope pills to feel a little tingle, so I can get on with things. Must make note to have minions step up drug addicting substances. I feel awful if I do not take these potions.

NOTE TO MINIONS: Stock up on controlled substances.

There must be a way to connect the soul to a body after they've died. This is the missing link I believe, to make Hell more Hellish. Bah. To think The Powers That Be can replace ME with a machine. I will drop Seeney another note today. MEMO: You can rely best on the Postal Service because unlike computers, nobody monitors or gives a shit what you send in your letters. Ha. Stupid silly humans. Shit do I feel like crap. Must take more drugs and put some food fuel in me. Maybe get another blowjob from prostitute, who is in the bathtub. I hope that I didn't kill her with all the fucking done before I pooped out. I need that blowjob before the drive. Oh yes, this driving is another fun thing to do. I am glad I took another vehicle from the truck stop. I must get on with my work.

I do not know how much longer the minions will be working for me if I do not come up with a good plan for Hell, but will maximize this crummy body before it dies of natural causes. Further note: The soul in this body is not worth sending to Hades. This is a moron's body. I can see the reflection in the mirror, and will be shopping for more clothing along the way. The prostitute told me I needed a tan, whatever that is, and will ask her if she is not dead. Maybe she will help me steal some "rays" whatever the fuck that is. She referred to this motel having a tanning parlor and pool. I do not have a lot of time according to the doctor, so I must get things done. The healer suggested this body is decaying with a condition that will need regular treatments. Ha. I do not have time for such silliness. Let it rot. Ha. There is distracting discomfort, and the pills make it easier to move. Other pills make the man part stick up like a sword. Ha.

The doctor, a Hebrew, was less than inclined to give me what I knew I needed for this earthly journey. I must point out: perhaps I was in violation of my Satanic chores by using my powers to influence him. To fill me up with all I needed. Make note: The Hebrews are particularly difficult to influence even when using full forces of evil.

No wonder they are rarely in Hades. At least the Catholics confess. I am certain if the Hebrews were indoctrinated—as a part of fulfilling the duties of their faith, to confess akin to the Catholics in the Confessional —it would make them more damnable and easier to influence. Ha. There were so many ways for me to infiltrate the human race. I have noted that the Hebrews rarely confess and imagine that if they did it would be in the presence of an attorney. Egads. It could be a complication in my plans to revamp my domain. Make note: Damn more Hebrews, and appoint a special commission in Hades upon my return to develop Hell's first Jewish community. Yes, there might be a way to undermine The Powers That Be from importing a new CEO of the netherworld. I will work on this. Cheers.

6 6 6

NOTE FROM EUSTICE

Hey Heathenistical friends this here's Eustice. I just got me a right fine notion. Lissen up: Satan's gonna git fired. I can't let that happen. They get to computerizin' Hades, or bringin' in some alien, Hell's gonna be a real mess. I gotta find some stuff to make Ole Mister Mephistopheles set all right, so he can fix up Hades to a place folk'll not particularly want to go to, but won't be run by some alien call center.

* * *

28

TRIP WILEY

So I get another call from Seeney, and he's got this hair brained plan to trick the Devil. How many more times is he going to fuss around with this crap. "Leave this shit alone already," I tell him. But no. It's NOT good enough, it's crucial "WE get involved," Eustice would say.

"What the fuck do you mean WE? Especially after the last debacle, huh?"

I've got to ask: Seriously why me again, helping Seeney deal with demons? I paid my dues a few times, and then some. Shit, now he's gotten in deep. This swapping letter shit? Penpals with Satan? Damn that's some funky shit, like prison pals. You don't know what you're dealing with.

Nonetheless I packed my bags, and told my girl we were going on a vacation. Some holiday, eh?

She was thrilled in that "How can I pack on short notice way," that's only resolved by saying you'll buy her a new wardrobe. Which the remains of Seeney's lawsuits would do. Make Luanne delighted to drop whatever it was she wasn't doing, and catch the next available flight out of Reno.

* * *

29

EUSTICE MEETS DOC WILEY AT THE HOTEL

The hotel sat grandly in Palm Beach, overlooking the ocean.

Knock, Knock. "Ya'all know that expression, don't ya?"

"When the Devil's at your door . . . ?" Wiley added. "Something like that. There's a quote by Oscar Wilde, goes like this: 'We are each our own devil, and we make this world our Hell.' It's pretty slick."

"Blah blah blah. He was some pansy. What'd he know but for nothin', writin' poetry and stuff. I don't reckon he ever done no dealin' with Ole Mephisto, do you?"

"Eustice, I can't say. But he sure did make it known."

"Collsarn groupies. You had that Martin Luther fella, the bull-pucky devil worshippers, the bible thumpers, you name it. All walks of life got their own notions. Hellfire.

Even the Good Book says some stuff about Satan. Says he wanted to be boss of Heaven. Got hisself kicked out."

"Yeah, yeah, I remember that shit." Wiley said.

"I know what I know, and I know ain't nobody gonna know our business dealin' with Satan. That's for sure. He gets a bad rep, it only makes Hell look crummier and crummier."

"Eustice, have you given any thought to the possibility that Satan may very well be tricking you with this so called visit' to earth?" Trip asked.

"Hell, yes."

"So?"

"I reckon iffen it's a trick, I'll bust his sorry ass but good."

"But you don't think it's a trick?" Trip responded.

"Nope. I saw how crummy of a place Hell was twice, and it'd got so politically correct there was no way eternal damnation could be as bad as it's supposed to be. Them folks from the old days wouldn't even know they was damned. Heck, they'd reckon they died and went to some promised land. Fact is Satan slouched, got lazy, and let too many minions fix the soup."

"Okay." Trip said

"I know what his gig's about. Now I'll tweak it a bit."

"When's he supposed to be here?"

"I don't reckon know. I think he's gonna mosey on down in whatever body he gets, and tool around earth. I gotta figure he got hisself a body nobody's gonna miss. One he could do earth things with, and one he can just shrug off."

"Makes sense."

"Doc Wiley, I want you to get a whole bunch of narcotics and stuff. Yep. That and maybe get some hookers and whores, and some regular gals rounded up."

"Why? How do you know Satan wouldn't take a female's body?"

"I gotta reckon he'd wanna test drive a johnson. You know why?"

"Why?"

"There's more folks got damned in all history from wieldin' their wanger like a weapon, than all the wars combined. Fellas been stickin' their johnson's in places since the first fella got the first boner."

"Oh shit." Wiley, who was sitting in a wooden chair crossed his legs, and rested his face in both palms. "Eustice, you want to make him feel human, right?"

"Yep."

"Women have sexual appetites Eustice."

"But they don't weaponize it, do they? Statistically they ain't got nary a candle to hold up to fellas done gone wild, pokin' this and that. That reminds me doc, we gotta get us some barnyard animals too."

"No Eustice." Wiley stood up and walked over to where Seeney sat on the sofa, a bottle of beer on the coffee table in front of him. "I draw the line somewhere."

"What line?"

"The line that says I'm not a pimp. Satan can find his own women."

"We're in this together Doc. Start to finish. We're gonna set this universe right. Go fetch yourself a cold one, and we'll round up some folks for a good party for Ole Mister Mephistopheles," Eustice said.

"I'm going back to my room Eustice. Call me when Satan shows up."

* * *

30

NOT A KNOCK KNOCK BUT SOMETHIN'S IN THE SWAMP

Home was a converted tour bus, purchased at a rest stop outside Orlando, Florida. Once a party on wheels for the roadie of a rock & roll band. A one-hit-wonder who'd blown their early 90s capital on: dope, cars, shenanigans, and this huge decoratively painted tour bus. Eustice had been living in hotel rooms since his big score, and wanted something he could: "Settle on into." Seeney had not lived an ordinary life by any means since his first brush with death, the afterlife, and subsequent malpractice suits. There were several out-of-court settlements, which set Seeney up well enough that he could afford to live as he pleased. He elected to keep on movin', on account "Satan or his minions'd be on my trail lookin' for me." Ultimately this angst passed, and neither Satan nor his minions took much interest in Eustice Seeney. After all, he died three times, going to Hell twice then to Heaven for a spell. Finally, he found himself cast back among the people of earth.

As it was Seeney's time had not yet come. Heaven, as The Powers That Be aptly stated, could wait. Eustice was busying himself watching some trial on cable television, sipping warm beer—alcohol free—noshing on Nacho Cheese Doritos, when he heard sounds on the deck. He had built it to surround his bus, which was located in a trailer park bordering the Everglades. The wheel's of the bus were removed as Eustice described: "I wanna take root here and let nature take it's course suroundin' my new home." Which is precisely what occurred. The massive tour bus, initially an eidetic epitaph to Heavy Metal Rap, was painted over with a matte black finish. Lush tropical flora had grown wildly over the stationary home of the man who'd crossed on over and faced the afterlife. It was, his neighbors would recall, one Hell of a dump. Seeney vociferously opposed any landscape manicure, as this would: "Be agin the forces of nature!"

The bus was located at the end of a cul-de-sac, on approximately 0.75 acres of overgrown land, owned wholly by the Eustice Seeney Foundation. An organization Eustice's legal counsel advised be established. As he did appreciate a degree of celebrity from the published accounts of his experiences.

The loosely knit community was not a homeowners association. Meaning to Seeney no quarterly maintenance fees, and no matching mailboxes.

The few neighbors on the street without streetlights, had a variety of cutesy mail receptacles.

Some flamingos, a few manatees, and the rest plain off the shelf el-cheapo little boxes. They all had a little red flag, indicating to the postal service that there was mail to be picked up, and mail delivered. As a corollary to this, none of the correspondence from Eustice to Satan could be traced anywhere but the dead letter file. This was one of Satan's little ploys. After all, the Prince of Darkness did have some pull at the post office. Rumor had it that he was most generous two days after Christmas. In some circles select employees got Anti-Christmas cards, while others got valuable gifts as well.

Seeney could walk out his door and enjoy the Everglades, and all that nature. Among the different types of plants in the Everglades are: palm trees, sawgrass, clumps of mangrove with twisted curling branches, hammocks, pine-lands, and what Briar Rabbit might call a great place to hide. There were gators, big ones, small ones, and all sorts of critters, that Eustice could listen to all night, gently soothing his haunted mind. Sawgrass is a common plant in the Everglades, found among the eight million acres of open flat prairie. It's one the toughest types of grass in the sedge family, and that's a family even the mangiest of bull gators didn't wrestle with. For Seeney, it was a barrier of sorts from outsiders, or curiosity seekers, who might catch a glimpse of the man who'd been there, done that, and came back to not shut up about it.

* * *

COULD IT BE THE POWERS THAT BE TRYIN' TO PLAY A TRICK ON ME?

Maybe Somethin' Else is up . . .

I swear I heard somethin' out back that tweren't no natural sound. It got me a bit spooked. Especially from that creep from Hell's bar, and the crummy contract letter. What the hey? I go look outside for anything out of the ordinary. It's daytime so I got me a good line of sight. I could see a whole lot from my back porch. Might pretty stuff too. Nature's just one fine thing to sit lookin' at. It goes on all day and night long, like it did all those years ago. Maybe time stays still for bugs and animals, and they don't know but for nothin' about time, or measurin' it. Never was a critter had a clock. I ought make a note of that. The Creator of the Universe must not of figured that important for dogs, caterpillars, armadillos, or even monkeys, to know what time it was. Maybe I ought run this by one of my pals, and come up with a special clock for non-humans. I'd have to reckon it'd have to be waterproof, for the manatees, dolphins, and fish. Yeah, now that I'm thinkin' about it, it'd have to be pressure proof too on account some fish swim real deep where the sun don't shine. Shee-yatt.

Here's another problem, I was gonna go solar powered, but that wouldn't work. Dang this invention business isn't easy stuff. I can't reckon how to get clocks into the hands, claws, tentacles, or whatever they'd have, to check time. Would their thinker brains work good enough for this? Maybe, maybe not. Way I get to figure is, that non humans go by the night and day schedule. Ain't got no calendars where they got seasons. Um-hmm, I think there's some way to do this, but not now. I gotta check out this place for minions. Look at that swamp, hoowee nothin' as natural as nature itself.

The mangroves made for swell places to hide out. And if Satan was comin' he may come by airboat through them. Smugglers brought in plenty of dope in the early seventies, of South Florida's drug days. There are three different parts of the mangroves, that bad guys of all sorts stretching back to pirate days, used.

I got to tell you that I didn't right know when Satan'd be here. And that minion, that sumbitch rat basserd, with the "Sport Business," had to make a big fuss with that collsarn letter to not tell nobody what he was up to. Bull-pucky. I got me a lawyer comin' by to set stuff right. I ain't goin' over to the city, on account some minion might try to bamboozle me. Maybe even somebody from The Powers That Be comin' `round here to smoke me out?

I don't know why, but I was real still starin' out there lettin' my thinker brain absorb stuff.

Gotta switch it off from inventin' critter clocks, but should write that down for later. Hang on, I think I see somethin' on one of the hammocks! I go fetch my binoculars and do a good look see.

Hardwood hammocks are sometimes described as tree islands. This is because they're small areas, and you find `em on the ground that's a little higher than the land surroundin' it. We got us some White-tailed Deer that sometimes hang out there. And come autumn after hurricane season, wild hogs feed there too. There's plenty of acorns and saw palmetto berries. Lots of other animals live in there: raccoon, bobcats, barred owls, hawks, and marsh rabbits. The hardwood hammocks are a Helluva places for animals. If you was plantin' stuff it'd grow real well too. The richest soil they say, is right here. Maybe some kids tryin' to grow weed out there. I best git my shotgun and fire a few shots, see if they go runnin', but not right now. Somethin's happenin' `round here, and I gotta check it out. Besides I can't find my collsarn shotgun. I figger maybe I'll just pull up my easy chair, put up my feet and gaze on out.

* * *

31

SATAN'S NOTE TO SELF

I am noticing this horrid mass of flesh is in constant need of fuel. The forms of which come in food products, some having effects on teeth, tongue, and swallowing. This human body nonsense is absurd. Whoever created this must have intended it to be fraught with repugnant sensations, and some I must confess somewhat delightful. That prostitute experience resulted in somewhat of an unusual tingling sensation from this retractable piece of flesh, which became firm and after several strokes emitted a very thick fluid. Hmm. This is curious, because other fluid comes from this several times per day, that is not as viscous.

I must say for lack of better descriptive words, delightful. After all those years not visiting earth I can almost see why The Powers That Be consider me "out of touch," which is no good at all. Now that I am here I get a sense of things.

Obviously some of these things are remarkable. Why? Because I can experience them, and using my highly refined, all knowing, universal intellect, make them horrid! I can sure use a drink—rather this rickety chunk of flesh can—some cigarettes too, and some of those "happy" pills. Maybe more of that sniffing powder that prostitute showed me. Yes, yes, yes. So many ways to wreck this body. Ha. No wonder many of these people who have been sent to me have cravings.

We already established that there is an afterlife. Derived by every electronic transaction a human is involved in throughout their life. Our life-file begins with each live birth, and since I spent the last few years building it, did not consider some of the very things I am experiencing.

Lord, Prince of Darkness, AKA for earthly purposes, Lewis Sifer

6 6 6

32

ME AND MR. MEPHISTOPHELES

I know Satan. That's right, ain't no question about it. Nope. Not one whatsoever. On account I done did die and go to Hell twice. That's right I been dead, and been eye to eye, nose to nose, with the Prince of Darkness, Lord of the Underworld, Lucifer himself. Yes, siree. I know my shee-yatt when it come's to demonagraphical science, and Hell's business. I know for certain how Satan went and used all modern technology up here on earth to amp up his game. Yep. Satan takes every keystroke, every website, every use of the computer, and compounds that with pictures. Pictures of everything you done did in your life, Satan has on file. Those cameras on the ceiling at the grocery store? Hell, they're piped into Satan's supercomputer. Banks, parking lots, all the places you ever been, is right there for Ole Mister Mephistopheles to use. Satan got every purchase of all the stuff you ever bought, every charge card swiped, all that cash you get from the ATM machine.

Hellfire, Satan got more poop on you than the spy agencies. If you got a number, Satan's got it. Based on my knowin' this stuff I can say in no uncertain terms: "That I can beat that ole Trickster at his own game." You know what that game is? I sure's fire do. It's to capture your eternal essence. Some folks call it a soul or spirit, and there ain't no scientific proof of that. Just like there ain't no proovin' what happens after you die.

However, there was this fella named Occam, and he had a theory that said: if you got a choice of a few things and can't make a decision, the easiest choice is usually the best way to go. Occam's Razor says that. So you may not be inclined to believe in an afterlife, not a lot of folks do, but they don't diss it. Some folks got a belief that there ain't nothin' but empty darkness when they croak. That's okay for them, but secretly they hope there ain't somethin' fierce. On the other hand, there's folks who're all full of the notions of Heaven and Hell. I know about Heaven, and tell you right off it ain't what folks imagine it to be. In fact, it ain't nothin' but a bunch of folks who ain't got no memories of ever bein' alive, floatin' around in some aether. It's stinky in that way. Hell's shitty too. You're in this place where all the rotten stuff in the world is replayed like a movie, over and over again for all time. I reckon it's different for some, on account I heard there's folks that like that. Personally they deserve a spot in Hades.

So that there's the preamble to my master plan. I don't reckon havin' a different sort of Hades is an improvement.

Hellfire, they go rearranging Hades they're liable to move the super bad folks—who're turfed on out to some outer space place—into the general population. Imagine that? Ordinary damned folks with bad credit scores, mixin' it up with terrorists, murderers, and worse?

Let me tell you this: Hell's neatly compartmented, so's the baddest of the bad get the crummiest hereafter. Sure the bad credit place is jam packed with so many folks I can't count that high. These are just your regular everyday crumbs like me and you. Miss a payment on your charge card, Boom. That goes on your to-be-damned list. Rob a bank? That's a whole different category of crime. There's sinnin', which pretty much are set in stone via them Ten Commandments.

Then there's the minor transgressions. You break one of the Big Ten, you get a higher Hell Score. But keep in your brain the fact that all violations of the Ten Commandments are negotiable. For instance, murder? They got wars, right? Self defense, right again. Stealin'? You got to feed your kids and swipe some shit, no big deal. Honor your folks? Think about some crazy ass parents and how that can be negotiated. Adultery? That was originally so women folk wouldn't go out and have other fellas babies. So that was brought before ancient Rabbinates. Those old Hebrews had this down to a science. Maybe that's why they have their own hereafter. There's such a thing as Justifiable Mistressism. Some marriages go straight to the pooper.

Well, if you catch my drift, the Big Ten C's can be interpreted in various ways. So there's some wiggle room at the Pearly Gates.

What happened on down the road was Satan sort of made new things sins, on account a lot of stuff wasn't invented in ancient times. Take that Gutenberg and his printing press. He went right to Hell. Why? Printin' the Good Book wasn't a sin, but he did a job for an Englishman. Over in olden times the King of England didn't want the people readin' the Good Book. So some smart fella had the idea to make money by bringin' the Book to the people for a price. He paid for it by goin' to jail on earth, and by extension so did the inventor. Sort of got complicated over the years.

Them painters in the Middle Ages? Straight to Hell. Pictures of bosoms and stuff. Nope, not so good.

Go back to them Templar Knights and how they was supposed to guard the road to Jerusalem for folks goin' to pay homage, or do some pilgrimage. But really dug tunnels and searched for the lost Secrets of King Solomon. Hellfire. Down in Hades some of the damned folks'd tell tales about Templars who'd made off with King Solomon's treasure, and lived out life on the beach havin' a good time.

Then they had the whole invention of the scientific method. That showed the earth to be round, and gravity and planets. That was a mess.

ME AND MR. MEPHISTOPHELES

Who was a charlatan and who was a scientist? Nobody right knew. But earth folks were happy to hand over people to Satan for eternity. Mind you this: humans can't damn other humans, but they CAN make recommendations. Since humans left the caves there was always someone ready to rat someone else out. That "Holier than" thing, it worked, and Hades got so jam packed Satan had to reach out to the folks. I think they'd be called folks even if they was non human from other planets—to warehouse all the souls he collected.

So the question I get asked a lot is: "How does the Devil power Hades?" He uses negative energy from all the souls he's collected. Albert Einstein explained it to me. Yep, he's in Hades—a Hebrew too—Satan made an exception for him, 'cause there's not too many great scientists, doctors, or lawyers in Hades. I'll get back to that.

Einstein got trapped by a technicality to land in Hell. No no no, it wasn't the A Bomb. It was from all the gals he was schtuppin'. He explained to me that Hades has a net negative charge. And his buddy, Max Planck—he's in Hell too—for that quantum theory business that explained how electrons work. Satan didn't want his secrets out, so he went out of his way to get him damned. Lots of historical folks in Hades. Isaac Newton, yep, that apple that fell on his head? He ate it. Satan got him on a technicality for poaching. The stealing gambit is one of Ole Mister Mephistopheles favorites.

So getting back to the mass giant negative charge, it keeps Hell cackling, zapping, and bippin' electrons here and there, sending signals that keeps the engines of Hades hummin'.

Makin' sure that the computers of Hell are runnin' in tip top form. Yep. Those supercomputers that Satan has are gettin' more data daily. And they can take up the exact opposite of all there is. You see Hell is the exact opposite of everything. Sort of a reverse universe. Say someone builds a building on earth, the same one goes up only upside down in Hell.

I heard somethin' outta the ordinary. Somethin' ain't right. I might be gettin' visited by a guardian angel or somethin'. Yep, that's always a possibility. Oh they exist if you get to wonderin'. Yes siree. But they ain't got no reason callin' on me. Heaven's sort of off limits for me these days, or is it?

I gotta think on this and maybe do some splainin' 'bout Heaven.

* * *

33

FOLKS THAT RAP ABOUT GOIN' TO HEAVEN

I got to depart from my preparatin' for Satan's impendin' visit, on account there's been a disturbance in the cosmic —collsarn does that sound dumb—plane. Yep. I heard some fella braggin' about how he done died and went to Heaven. Ordinarily I'd just shake my head and blow it off, but when I read that this guy might be fibbin' I got worked up. I mean real worked up.

This fella was supposed to be some big shot doctor, who claimed to been in a coma, and went to some "other place." Blah blah blah. He made such a big deal out of it, that all the big shots of the world took notice. He was all over the TV, news, and bestseller lists. I did some research and looked into this fella. Who knows? Maybe he had a legit deal, right?

It turns out he been sued a bunch of times, did some funny stuff in the doctorin' world, and got himself booted from his cushy job.

He was probably stuck on Satan's treadmill, keepin' up with keepin' up. Yep. See it all the time. Folks get all caught up in a certain way of life and get lost. I studied this remarkable yarn that was all over the place: Big shot doctor scientist saw the light, and proves there's Heaven.

Proves there's Heaven? Hang on a minute. He may of seen some light, but that light was a spotlight on that colored ladies TV show. He was a regular superstar advertisement for Heaven. Every place I looked there was more and more people pontificatin' on this real educated fella. An ivy league doctor scientist, who: "Saw the light." I read so much about it I got dizzy. All the sappy stuff fat ladies with upside down glasses and dogs on their laps, praise Jesus about, when they're stuck in traffic. The true believers shot down anyone questionin' this fella. The cynics tossed in their skepticism about how a brain stays alive after death, blah blah blah. But looky here, you cannot ever convince a true believer that they might be gettin' bamboozled, on account they laid out twenty maybe thirty bucks for this: Afterlife Porn.

That's what I call these near death, afterlife folks who push their experiences, the way a dope dealer sells crack. But this fella, a big shot doc, took it too far. He was flauntin' fake fables to make bank.

I got to tell you that I felt like throwin' up every time someone mentioned how wonderful this charlatan was. Between you and me, there ain't no chance this fella's gonna EVER see the Pearly Gates.

I'll ask Satan when he gets here. Probably has a chamber in Hades ready and waitin' for him. This boy is goin' straight to Hell. Imagine a fella claiming there's butterflies in Heaven?

The more I read the more I felt compelled to save poor schnooks from gettin' involved with a soon-to-be minion of Satan himself. I heard a bell ring when I discovered this evil doin' man. A doctor who operated on the wrong parts of people. A doctor who'd not only been sued, but got sneaky and changed his records so he didn't have to pay his due. Hoowee. This is real sin city shadoobie. Hell, that is where this fella went. He's claimin' that there's all sorts of beautifully colored clouds and butterflies in Heaven, blah blah blah.

Well Buddy: THERE Ain't NO BUTTERFLIES in Heaven, and the place is boring as kissin' your cousin. That's the Devil's doin'. There's somethin' not right here. Somethin' is astir. I gotta check it out now.

* * *

34

SATAN'S LOG: EARTH DATE #6

I awoke today in a vehicle with my notes. This body is not only foul smelling, there is excrement all over the clothing at both the front and back side. I have been driving a vehicle.

I am truly in a farrago of fools. Human folly, insufferable idiots, whose souls my charge is to obtain, has become more ineffective lately. The former generations of mankind would be sent into a state of extreme anxiety, nervousness, or distress; the fantods. Ha. How I love the sense of fright. The fantods of the feeble, anticipating demonic presence. I could make a human soil themselves by the mere mention of my name. Now I am—according to the PTB—a feckless old fool of fairy tales. A has-been from Hell. My frightening foiled by humanly games. Now I shall put an end to this folderol. I shall in the form of a human, bring terror back into the name of Satan. I will— in this shoddy human form—Resurrect Fear. Ha.

ME AND MR. MEPHISTOPHELES

I have been driving for hours, sans the sleep thing humans cherish so much. I have no need for this. Yet I know the body does in order to sustain, just as it does food. So its appearance is shocking.

I await the faces of humans: men, women, and children alike. When I enter the rest stop and feed this heap of flesh and organs. This rotting mass of tissues. If I can find it revolting, and this is nothing, the humans will have fits. I am sitting here smoking more cigarettes, and waiting for the pills to take hold. I brought the prostitute with me. I do not recall her name. Why should I? She's a well paid servant, whom I have given human sleep medicine to. Using my powers of Satanic influence: hypnotized, mesmerized, and yes, taken this street whore along with me to do my bidding. This is not anything a human would find odd, as I have even put a uniform on her so she appears to be an ordinary working woman. Ha. I look like a well heeled gentleman with his "girlfriend." Perhaps adorning her with jewels, which I can toss about like pebbles. At least until my time here is done.

6 6 6

35

SEVEN DAYS ON EARTH

Perhaps I did not state this initially, so will insert it here. I was given a humans week to create a new Hell. That is correct. The PTB were quite clear. They said that the Creator of the Universe had 7 days, actually 6, and one to rest. So I have a week to remind the universe that I am the true ruler of all things evil. By the serpents of the darkest deepest dungeons, where the most vile wretches scream out in agony, I shall prevail as Lord and Ruler of the Underworld. Not now, not ever, to be queried as to my absolute ability to reign Hell. Ha. I'll have another Kool, wake the whore, and feed this piece of crap of a body. Maybe I took the wrong pill . . . something's happening.

It is clear that I will not be able to garner all the material required to complete my mission in this body, and must file an appeal to The Powers That Be.

ME AND MR. MEPHISTOPHELES

I have sent out a demonic signal using a call center in a Far East location. Earth dwellers have no idea how many of these "call centers" we, Hell that is, own and routinely bring aggravation to. In fact many of the team leaders and supervisors are already damned. Merely awaiting their body's expiration date to join Hell's general population. Amazing what some earth people will do for a little bit of money.

That brings to mind a passage in one of the humans religious books. To paraphrase a man not Hell-worthy: "Money is the root of all evil," Ha. If he only knew what people sold their souls for.

6 6 6

36

DON'T HATE THE PLAYER

I'm settin' back waitin', bein' as still as I can. Takin' in nature in all its naturalness. And I get to thinkin' thoughts.

Lot's of folks hate this or that based on some unconscious stuff there ain't no accountin' for. But that ain't right. Everybody: that goes for robots, aliens, and Satan too, gotta have some respect for the game itself. The game I'm talkin' 'bout here is the game of life. Life ain't always what you think it's gonna be, but in the long run it's all you got. Sometimes you gotta reckon history as somethin' you really must take into account.

For instance, line up a human persons life span to say eighty years, from birth till death. Do the arithmetic and see. I'm not too good on this without a calculator. Eighty years ago . . . what was goin' on in this world?

ME AND MR. MEPHISTOPHELES

Tweren't no internet. Nope. No phones like we know `em. In fact, the first phone call was March 10, 1876. A bit more than 240 years ago, around there someplace. I can't find my calculator. Another thing that wasn't no place to be bought till 1972. Collsarn whole bunch of shee-yatt we take for granted in this day and age, that wasn't around even twenty years ago!

Kids born after 2001 are used to bein' fanny handled at airports, snooped on, and aware that bad guys wanna do crummy things. Hellfire. More happened in one life span: from WW II, Nazis, Jetliners, Facebook, Twittering, TV shows, and things that make you get the heebie-jeebies, jimjams, and willies thinkin' about.

I know as a fact that Satan had his hand in a lot of the technological innovations. The Satanical Supercomputer bein' plugged in as it is. Every collsarn keystroke a human makes is common knowledge to those of us been damned, and matter-of-fact to us Hell regulars. Eighty years'd make America a very new place. Yes siree. In the overall scheme of the universe, the US of A is just a blip on the cosmic screen.

So you got to take a step back to sum up your strategy when you get a call from the Devil. And he's gonna come a callin'.

Satan has been at this game since humans left the cave. That'd be maybe what 900 eighty year life spans ago?

That Ole Coot Satan been around a long time. He knows what makes us humans tick, and what buttons to push. How we lie, cheat, steal, and screw. Ain't no dummy. However, just because he's been around don't make him infallible. Satan's got a job to do, and that's to take that energy field we call a soul, and move it across the board into his corner.

The Powers That Be, who created this universe, set up Satan as a challenge. The Powers created man in their image, which I interpret to be creative. Simple as that. You get to be born, you got one purpose. You do creative stuff and follow the rules the PTB sent on over.

The PTB sent down "Commandments," that although lots of folks think are engraved in stone, are negotiable rules. That's how lawyers and scholars of the law got started.

"Thou shalt not kill," was a biggy on account there was wars, and Satan'd argue through one of Hell's lawyers that he owned a soldier's soul. The PTB'd say war was part of the human experience. "Thou shalt not steal," was another biggy, Satan'd get all excited about. The Powers'd make exceptions for hungry or starving families. That'd drive Ole Mister Mephistopheles nuts.

Down the road on into this eighty year lifespan, Satan invented credit scores, and that stumped The Powers. Satan set it up just so he could lay claim to a soul if they had a bad credit score. Somethin' real important about The Powers That Be, they always played it fair.

As much as Satan finagled, maybe tried to fudge the evidence, tweak the rules, he HAD to play by the rules. Satan's game is: Eternity's Dispensation of the Human Soul. So like I said, you can hate the players, but you can't hate the game.

Things were runnin' pretty smooth on through the Roman Empire. A batch of souls here, a batch there. There was a balance in the universe. How many lifetimes ago was that? Twenty plus lifetimes, maybe? I told you I don't have my calculator. But Satan was there. There was some serious crummy stuff in: SPQR. That's how they spelled Rome back then. But there was a fall of the Roman Empire, and it was because there was funky stuff goin' on. Satan was there rakin' souls in so fast he started gettin' lazy.

Before that: the Egyptian Pyramid builders, Mayans, Incas, and those fellas who built that big Ole Wall of China. Take it from me, there's plenty of Chinamen souls in Hades. I think Satan had an appetite for the Mu Shu Chicken, and Sweet and Sour Shrimp, when he'd take to explorin' the terrain. He'd pop into someone's body on occasion, but it'd only be for a brief spell, never a few days.

The rules were set. The deal with Satan was that The Powers That Be sent one of their own. An entity to run the show for the damned. On the topic of the other place. The Powers send folk's souls to? I been there. And yes, there are things that happen after the body dies.

I told that story in "Forheavenstake" through the guy who made me up.

So Heaven does exist. In fact, it ain't all it's cracked up to be. It's detailed in that tale. Nonetheless that's not why we're here. If Satan loses his gig as the boss of the underworld somebody or somethin' will surely replace him, and nobody could imagine who or what that would be. Can you think of letters of the alphabet beyond Z? I can't.

So with that knowledge and my own personal experience of Hell, Heaven, and how history's been arranged, it's obvious there's a lot more that's gonna happen in the next 80 years. Hellfire, I'm pert near the halfway mark, and humans are still doin' dumb ass shit. Only with fancier gadgets, better detergents, and nifty plumbing to boot. Now I got to figure this out. Still can't remember where that collsarn calculator is.

* * *

37

SATAN'S NOTE

That nincompoop Seeney is going to attempt a coup. Ha. What a fool. I will be ready for anything he has waiting for me. This buffoon's twisted ways immunize him from much of my influence. Once I pin him down I may discover the missing link in what the PTB found lacking in my work. I believe that maintaining a connection to the living body and its sensory system might just be the ticket. Hmm. This will require use of my IT department from earth's Hades, to those outside this solar system. Hmm. Perpetuating pain for all eternity has a nice ring to it. Keeping the body connected forever could be a real innovation for an eternal damnation. I just have to rig it up.

6 6 6

38

EUSTICE

Mind you now, I was just settin' in my easy chair doin' a good think, when that tingly feeling comes over me again. A might more intensificated. And just like that I hear a clack clack clack. Somebody's here.

I grabbed my ball bat, Louisville Slugger, I keep next to the front door, and opened `er on up real slow listenin' to the door's creak. The sound drowned out the crickets, cicadas, and the woodpecker that's usually drivin' me nuts, finally just shut the heck up. Somethin' WAS up. All nature seemed to hush up when I had the door full open, weapon in hand, ready to take on whatever it was. The sun tweren't hardly over the Dade Pines across the road. Not a cloud in the sky, and it was already pert near ninety degrees. Today was gonna be a scorcher. There was no breeze, and the air was thick as mayonnaise. Each breath hurt my chest as I moved on down to the end of my driveway.

My vehicles weren't scratched, no windows broken—a good sign—as I tiptoed toward that box. Dang, I oughta cement my driveway, collsarn gravel was diggin' into my feet like tiny razor blades. I was so jittery I forgot to put on my boots. It seemed like each step I took it got quieter and quieter. Shee-yatt it felt like I was the only livin' critter in the Glades. Even my neighbor's pit bull wasn't barkin'. Which was sort of nice really, on account that sumbitch is noisy as an ex-wife when a payment's due. I kept movin' till I got to the box. I reached out real slow, and I reckon—as a matter of habit—lowered the flag and put my thumb and finger together on the latch. I was just about to give it a tug, when BAM!

The flap shot open like a jack-in-the-box, and sent me flyin' back. I was so freaked out I swear I'd had a heart attack. I think I froze for a spell. This wasn't no cherry bomb. Somebody or something did somethin' to make this mailbox act up like this. It seemed like it was possessed!

Eustice, I said to myself, comport yourself like a gentleman without fear. You done died and gone to Hell, and beat the Devil at his game. Not once but twice. You died and went to heaven too! There ain't nothin' in all creation you should fear, right? But I'll fess up, I was spooked. Nature must've agreed, on account the lush ecosystem I lived in was usually more alive than a cathouse full of horny hookers on a Saturday night. Complete silence.

I was just sittin' there on the ground, a regular nervous Nelly, when all of a sudden the wind kicks up. It blows through the tops of the trees that get to swayin', and the sound is like the ocean rushin' up on shore loud. Kinda like all nature is a wind instrument bein' played by the breeze, blowin' some foul breath through 'em. Finally I stand up and look inside the box. I felt a jolt of the willies. Yep, that's like heebie-jeebies times ten, in the form of white hot lava passin' through me. Holy shee-yatt! I knew Satan was a lookin' at me square in the thinker brain. Satan could see into my soul, don't ask me how I know, but there's some things I just collsarn do! I stood up at attention like the ghost of General George Patton was standin' right in front of me. With that cattwompin' ridin' crop ready, set, and hankerin' to slap me silly.

I heard voices in the bushes. Sounded like little kids tellin' secrets. That tweren't no kids. It was either Satan or his minions up to no good. I wasn't gonna let that happen, no siree. That rascal had no business without my permission. I was steamin', and went into a thrashin' the hedges like a windmill in a tornado, my Louisville Slugger tight in my hands. My eyes open bigger than a hooker's cooter on Sunday morning after the fleet's left town. I can't but barely speak, and my hands get to shakin' somethin' fierce, then everything just went black.

* * *

39

SATAN'S LOG: OBSERVING HUMANS

Watching human beings is indeed compelling. I find myself lost in thoughts as I observe, and do some dwelling. Alas! There do exist so many fresh faced fools. A farrago of fantods. I feel it in my flesh, a feeble mass of rubbish that's truly human trash. I know they'll falter, fail, and strive, as long as they are alive. The folly, greed, and cruelties unbidden, become the fodder for my den. I await as they arrive.

My minions remain somewhat loyal as I have absolute power of my domain. How could they know there was an axe being wielded by The Powers? No. I needed to stifle Seeney, to keep him misdirected. Dread, fear, self-doubt, and questioning himself is one of my specialities. I most certainly will keep him walking a post until I arrive. Ha.

40

TRIP WILEY ARRIVES

I found Eustice laying on his back. A baseball bat, five maybe ten feet away. He soiled his jeans and his shirt was soaked. Sweat? Probably. It was noon and the day's heat had me beginning to pour out sweat. My car thank goodness, had fresh air conditioning coolant thanks to Seeney. He paid for my trip down here. Yippee, Sunny Florida. Again with this devil shit. I missed Vegas and my gig working part time again as a physician. I still had some issues with the state board, not insurmountable, but I had my fair share of spare time. Doing a bit of Elvis tribute work kept me in shape. That's where I met Luanne, who was watching from the rental car. I was glad she agreed to come with me. I motioned for Luanne to join me, as I didn't know if Seeney was injured. So I used the fireman's carry.

The technique is commonly used by firefighters to carry injured or unconscious people away from danger. I didn't know what was wrong with him.

The technique has since been replaced in the firefighting community. The drawbacks of smoke and heat are greater higher up, and could be fatal. I didn't have far to go to get him into his rig. If we weren't at sea level maybe I would have gotten the wheelbarrow Eustice had parked up the driveway. I looked around, checked the terrain for unfriendliness. Nothing, not even a gator just an unconscious Eustice Seeney and nature. I checked his vitals, he was going to live. Something must have stunned him. Maybe his electrolytes were off. I didn't know, but I didn't think I'd have to call 911. I took a deep breath, bent my knees, and put my arms around him. He was either heavier than I imagined, or gravity was playing tricks on me, but I managed to get him up on my shoulders. The "fireman's carry" is an effective technique. Even my gal could have done this. It's still taught for use outside of firefighting. Soldiers use this technique to carry wounded comrades. Lifeguards are sometimes trained to use the fireman's carry too. I've seen dainty little girls schlep a wiped out surfer across the beach when I was growing up in Southern California, so I knew I wouldn't be risking a hernia. As if I needed any more grief. This trip really cut into my style. I did after all have a life to live, and things were heating up with Luanne.

* * *

41

LUANNE

Luanne Jennifer Robey (shortened from Rubislavic) left Akron, Ohio seven years earlier for Los Angeles. The acting career she aspired to did not work out as planned. Maybe it was her inability to recall lines, or the persistent vertigo that made her stumble from time to time. The casting calls did not go well. Maybe it was only a select few, very few, who realized her skills as an actor. "You are truly gifted," that's what her first coach said. Acting was her "calling." The man who appreciated her most, Mr. Tuttleburger, was her acting teacher at Akron High. He not only fancied the spray of freckles across her face, and that cute tattoo on her ankle—maybe it was a birth mark —he never knew or cared, because most of his dermatologic attention vectored in just above her pert breasts. Occasionally wandering downward when he helped her strike a pose. He spent extraordinary periods of time just standing in place behind her holding her just so, and positioning her like some mannequin.

ME AND MR. MEPHISTOPHELES

Lance Tuttleburger spent hours after school tutoring Luanne on the finer points of enunciation, thus eliminating her midwest accent. He enjoyed the lilac scent of her not quite adult, although mature figure. As his parole officer would recall: his description of Luanne's décolletage kept him pissing in a cup long after she left for greener pastures. His collection of photographs from hidden cameras throughout the school proved awkward among the county prosecutor's office. He would most certainly perish in prison. The photos, the ones they found, were not exactly that revealing. Then again, if they found his secret stash he may have been explaining his fascination with Tennessee Williams on a prison yard.

Nonetheless, her mother, Lola Robey, did not object to her daughters journey west. Leaving Akron was just the ticket, her mom thought. Especially after her daughters daily detailed discomfit in the presence of her acting coach. The tipping point was when Mr. Tuttleburger placed both palms on her shoulders in a run through of the school play: "The Glass Menagerie." His role, "The Gentleman Caller" did somewhat more to Luanne's character "Laura," than simply brush past a glass unicorn, knock it to the floor, and break off its horn. This may not have been the end of Luanne's youth, but it certainly marked the beginning of the end of her teachers career. Mr. Tuttleburger failed to notice the Assistant Principal of Akron High looking on, as he fondled Luanne in a manner unscripted by the playwright.

No, Tennessee Williams did not include that scene in the 1944 premiere of his play. The Akron police department agreed. Mrs. Robey's former husband, Jules, drove in from nearby Columbus where he worked as a night watchman at the Ohio State University: to pay child support, and drink daily to mourn his lost youth, expanding waistline, and lament over his medical condition. Dr. Sorenberg, the OSU Dermatologist, determined the "freckle on his schmekel" would result in partial amputation of his penis. Jules agreed the teen would thrive in Los Angeles, where her Aunt Donna had a position open at an antique shop in the San Fernando Valley. Donna needed someone to look after the shop while she did part-time tarot card readings.

Aunt Donna owned a deck brought over from the "old country," and if she dealt them in front of a client "just so," she could make up any story she wanted. The sucker, client that is, would pay nicely. Oddly whatever fortune Donna told had a way of being roughly accurate. Maybe it was Donna's skill at sizing people up, as in the car they drove up in, their jewelry, their accent. Whatever it was Donna had the gift of gab. If anything brought folks into an antique shop in one of the nation's largest array of strip malls it was the spiel she could lay on. The words: "Tarot Readings," in the window were enticing, but it was indeed a rare deck. Just how rare Donna didn't know. She only shared her prized possession, the Visconti-Sforza Deck with a few people. Some folks thought she could really toss a mean reading, especially in the Valley.

It was complete bullshit because she knew her prized deck was missing a few cards. She made up for it by embellishing her way through a reading. It being a 15th Century relic, her uncle passed on to her via the crumbling Balkan ruins of the later part of the last century. The tattered cards had been through some bombing raid. She could rattle off all sorts of details that sounded legit. Her spiel went something like this: "The Visconti-Sforza deck is one of several hand-painted Italian decks. The Visconti family, our cousins, were commissioned back in the 15th Century to design the deck, when they left Romania. It may or may not be older than the famed Cary-Yale Visconti deck."

The woman could bullshit, and clients would be dazzled as she proceeded: "I don't know for sure how old these cards really are, but they have powers. This deck has 74 of the original 78 cards, the missing cards are The Tower, The Three of Swords, the Knight of Coins, and The Devil. Some of these cards are fading, but don't worry I can read into them, my Romanian blood and all. Look at them, like all Tarots of the Visconti lineage, these will portend what befalls its special circumstances to each individual as they're dealt. 'Look' she'd tell the client in a dimly lit room in the back of the antique shop. The cards speak in their order of display as I place them before you. As you see they are unnamed and unnumbered. Only I can read their message."

Even her sister thought it sounded cool. Cool enough for her daughter to find a way into Hollywood.

This job opening sounded great to Luanne's mother, a full time hash slinger at Denny's. An ideal way to live the life she wanted, and continue her clandestine affair with Denny's regional manager. As well as contribute to her daughter's not-quite college aspirations. Lola was not naive to the the Valley. She spent four years there after leaving home herself, as an adult performer in at least twenty custom videos. Featuring some steamy albeit unnatural relations with other adult actors, formerly known as porn stars. "Honey," Lola said to Luanne five years ago, "There's no future for you in Akron." And so it goes.

Six months of L.A. led to a severe cocaine jag, a traffic stop, and being released from her job selling antiques by day, and working the club scene by night. Never getting farther than the casting couch. Vegas was an option Aunt Donna suggested, and she knew just the right cocktail lounge. A lounge favored by none other than Dr. Trip Wiley. They had been seeing each other for nearly six months she reflected, as she watched Trip carry Eustice into the immense mobile home. She had a general idea that this all expense paid trip to South Florida was on this redneck, stumble bum's ticket. She did find it hard to believe this guy actually died and went to Hell . . . twice. But she had no question her beau, Doc Wiley, was any less than the real deal. After all, he did promise to remove the tattoo on her ankle. So she felt pretty good about that. Maybe she ought to go inside and help.

42

Aunt Donna's antique shop specialized in kitsch. With the pinkest of pink flamingo inventory, plenty of velvet paintings: bullfighters, Elvis, Jesus, and a gold lame trinket trove for lovers of tackiness. Those who'd wandered off the Sunset Strip in search of goodies to adorn their faux castles. The Valley, home to the porn industry, so-so dining, cheesy strip malls, and anything most middle American's would find reprehensible; in fact crappy about Southern California. Spend a few hours in the smog filled San Fernando Valley. Yup, that'll do it. The traffic is bumpa-ta-bumpa on most days. The nights are filled with cars adorning altered fuck ups, with more DUIs and STDs than any other consecutive set of three letters in their lexicon. The DUI had been a badge many Valley folk wore on their bumpers. Next to the Support Your Local Sheriff stick-on, the Peace Sign, and Elect Romney—over the Obama campaign stickers.

Miles and miles of strip malls, Chiropractors, sushi dives, nail salons, supermarkets—of a name-that-ethnic group, for miles on end. Every stoplight was a potential road-rage setup, or a scene from a coming to a theatre near you locale. That was just the surface of this delightful part of Southern California. Many of the topless bars along the Ventura Highway were filled with day drinking, hard grinding, working folks. Those with a gig doing a condom covered shoot—depending on how high the yen was, for something new, something fierce, something that'd rock the world. Every waiter, waitress, and paperboy had a script to sell. And the car next to you at the red light might just be the next Scarlett what's her name.

L.A., The City of Angels. Smack dab where Aunt Donna opened her shop. Sadly for Donna she didn't know shit about antiques. She did like to make money and have some fun. Donna's shop was also a medical office of sorts —the sort you don't visit when you're sick, rather when you want to feel better than okay. She shared space with Zill Crapmonger, Osteopath to the stars. "Yup yup." That's what she came to say after every sentence. Picked it up from Zill. "Yup, yup."

Formerly of Brooklyn, Zill, attended the Still College of Osteopathy. He did a one year internship followed by a residency in Anesthesiology. He hated it. Hospitals, passing gas, watching monitors, and opened up shop as a "pain specialist" in the San Fernando Valley. He knew his drugs, and had the bona fides to dole them out.

ME AND MR. MEPHISTOPHELES

Of course there were a few incidents at Bumfuck Osteopathic General that caused a stir with the state board, but fuck it. There was easy bank to be made, and plenty of it. He'd begun his career as a true believer in Osteopathic theory, and Osteopathic manual manipulation. But there were five Chiropractors to every fifty people, and he had to spend four years in medical school. A legit residency beat being a family practice doc, hence the residency gone sour.

When the smoke cleared he had a valid prescription pad, and the writing was on the wall at every pharmacy in the Valley. Doling out narcotics to porn stars in the days of disco. That pre-Viagra era needed a doc on the spot, who'd shut the fuck up if John-Q showed up. Hey the laws the law, and this wasn't Studio City. Yup yup. Junkies, in that sterile legit sort of way, could see a board certified doc for their daily fix. "This was the Valley baby," where legit was a four letter word. Years before the Galleria Mall closed, the place was happenin'. But that all came to a halt with the AIDS wave. That shut down even the most unwholesome of glory holes, whore houses, and funk that seemed to lace the smog.

Ah the memories, Zill'd reflect, adjusting his toupee and playing with his coke spoon necklace. He was listening to the piped in BeeGees when Donna presented the notion of sharing office space. "An antique shop? Yup yup that's cool, I can do that. Yup yup." In fact, Zill's office was filled with so much leftover crap from the stagnant porn industry he could've opened a used furniture store—a very stained one at that too.

The props originally came from the major studios across town. Get rid of the crap: the execs at Paramount, Universal, and the Brothers Warner said. Junk that spanned history for authenticity in film. Predating computer generated graphics, and much cheaper constructing props right there on set. So Donna and Zill Crapmonger had a healthy, unwholesome relationship. Porn had a rebirth after the cootie doom days. Pill cocktails, cooked up by the world's greatest docs, and Zill had the ticket to dole them out. Business picked up with AZT, but really amped up with the combo drugs, to set HIV positive folks with long lives and prosperity. So much for that. Zill and Donna were in a funk as the Valley's golden days seemed over. All wasn't lost because Zill could still do his doctoring in that—eww-legit way. Zill wasn't exactly attuned to caring for the sick. He was more the skin of your pants, seat of your hoofs kind of way. So they struggled, and the Osteopathic antique shop for aging not-so B actors scraped by.

Osteopaths are real docs, but Zill quite simply was a quack. Looking for any shortcut, any time, any where. When the big bug was held at bay, and porn went mainstream, Zill went to doling out dope to the stupid. There was a miracle brewing thanks to technology, cheap filming, and a tweak of one simple biochemical pathway. Zill, was back in biz! Yippee. Viagra and a mess of other get-high drugs went wild. It was like every slot machine in Vegas hit a win at once. There were lines around the block waiting for one of Zill's prescriptions.

Money, money, money, thanks to cock-propping, wonder penis pills. Who could resist serial blow jobs, hand jobs, and rim jobs. After the real estate crash and market frenzy, Zill miraculously skated like Dorothy Hamill, and had the gold medal to show for it. Yup yup. Zill was reflecting on life, death, his dick, and how Donna's tits were sagging, and maybe springing for a lift. When the phone rang.

Who the fuck calls on this line? Zill said, as he listened.

"Luanne?" he asked.

"Hi, is my aunt around?"

"It's me, Dr. Crapmonger, you know your aunt's . . ."

"I know all about you," Luanne replied.

"What might you know cupcake, huh?" Zill was in no mood, not now, not ever, to take any shit from a broad. Especially a chick who passed up a solid career as a porn performer. Sure she'd have to show her fluffer skills, but no, the little chippie would have made a damn decent pole dancer. Fucking broads.

"Just get my Aunt Donna or—"

"Or what cupcake?" Zill loved busting the chops of little chippies, this one especially, and her nice little rack. He was just feeling a nice wave of tumescence, when Donna grabbed the phone from him.

"Give me the phone creep." Donna saw his hand on his crotch, and said "Go take a cold shower you pig. This is family, not one of your moron 'stars' Zill." She grabbed the phone, "Hello honey."

Donna pressed the phone hard to her ear, so Zill couldn't hear what her niece was saying. But Zill knew by Donna's pacing, the arm across her chest, the pallor in her face, whatever that niece with nice knockers needed, it was important. Zill Crapmonger was never a man unwilling to rise to the occasion, as a white knight to save the day. Nothing like being a hero, especially if there might be something in it for him. Why else would the little ho call from Vegas unless she was in a jam? He listened and watched. He sensed a score.

Donna paced as she spoke, listening carefully to her sisters daughter. After all, the orange and yellow glow of the Denny's next door didn't have a "help wanted" sign beneath it, and there was no way she could move back to L.A. She glanced at Zill's faux innocent eyes, angelically staring at Donna as he fidgeted with his gold medallion, letting it drop to his gray fuzzy haired chest. Smoothing his hair piece, he held his hand up pinky ring finger and thumb mimicking a phone, mouthing: "Have her come here we'll put her up."

Donna looked at the Osteopath to the stars with a gaze reserved for shoplifters, pedophiles, and folks who'd make any no-fly watch list.

Luanne initially did not want to join Trip on his journey. She'd heard about Eustice Seeney. Now her aunt said it was "in the cards," meaning to Luanne that Aunt Donna thew the tarot on her. Oh she hated it when Aunt Donna did that. Ever since she was a little girl in Akron, Aunt Donna would deal those stinking cards, and tell everyone's future. If she could tell any future a few winning lottery numbers wouldn't hurt, would they? Aunt Donna did say that Seeney was trouble, more than she cared to even get involved in. She said the cards were sending her mixed messages. Luanne wrote it off in her mind as absolute bullshit, but she was kin, and had to be polite. Florida with Trip and this wacky guy who went to Hell? Omigosh. Her parents would die if they knew.

* * *

43

ORLANDO

SATAN AT DISNEY WORLD

Earth Day Seven

I awoke today with a new woman. She arrived in the middle of the night. I did not order a whore. I would imagine the Indian man at the check-in was being hospitable, as I paid him a week's pay for one night. Ha. Perhaps when I asked if there were any "diversions" for a gentleman on the road he used his human imagination. Thinking all of us humans simply wanted meat. Tenderloin meat. Ha.

What a night in Orlando.

Ha. The powers indeed relented. Alas another day among the humans. But this forsaken flesh and its needs to merely move. Pills for this and that, the fluids, solids, and fuels. So joyful to use some parts, and foul odors for others. I must make a note: Construct some olfaction in the chambers of Hades.

Nonetheless, I have arrived at a most popular theme park in a ridiculous swamp terrain, with mice and dogs, and rides and long lines. Ha. If the fools only knew from lines.

The Day's Inn hotel: I must make note to have the minions contact these people. A night at one of these is so much like home, every damned human should stay there at least once. The paper over the porcelain bowl makes a fine target to express the solid matter—stools. Ah yes. So wonderful. The collection of medications to make this damn thing stop coughing, move the arms and legs, make its mind think as I wish, Egads. The little treats my prostitute friends bring me, Delightful. I must make note: that I am uncertain what to do with these trollops once finished, lest I commit some transgression of earth laws. Fortunately my minions are just a few thoughts away, but the drugs dull my powers. Like my little playthings say: You can't always get what you want. Ha. Of course I can.

I awoke on this day with a new whore, and we went through every possible sex act humans can do. Make note: Stop using human body when the flesh becomes bloodied and raw. Oh well. A trip she suggested to the land of the mouse was in order. Note: These prostitutes who will ultimately be rewarded in Hades, have no names. I cannot bother with names for these flesh buckets. Just along for the ride ladies. Ha. I am getting the lingo very well.

Off to Disney, then to that nincompoop Seeney in the swamp. Ha. Maybe I will bring him one of my women. But first I need to message him to prepare for my arrival. I will give him a list detailing all I need. I have been experiencing some difficulty in obtaining some of my most favored narcotic drugs, and the cancer medicines are making this body vomit, and clumps of hair fall out. Ha. Clumps of hair. What a fine sight for new arrivals in Hell to see: pieces of their bodies falling off. Maybe I will have finger or toe removed to see how long it bleeds. Blood. What a silly filling. It would have been so much easier for the Creator to have simply used sea water. I need some happy pills.

Lewis Sifer, the hooker would later recall, was a real doozy of customer. But those trips to the ATM machine made her Pimp smile. This was a new pimp, a big black man. The substitute for her usual pimp. The hooker didn't really care because this new pimp, the one who set her up with this freak, was letting her keep ALL the money. Sort of a new management perk.

6 6 6

44

LUANNE'S REVERIE

Once they were on board the 727, Trip put his hand on Luanne's upper thigh, squeezed the lithe flesh beneath her jeans, and said: "Luanne, this is going to be fun. We're going to enjoy ourselves. I know you're not into this, but give it a chance."

"Why do we have to stay at HIS place? Why can't we stay on South Beach, or a nice hotel?"

"Honey," Trip took a sip of his drink. The second ten dollar mini the air host had given, after the second hour in the flight, after the second layover. Three sets of two . . . did that mean anything? Nah. "It's going to be fine. Once we're done with the business with Eustice we'll take a ride up to Palm Beach. You can meet my grandparents, maybe spend some time on the island. Relax, it'll be fun."

She put her hand over his, squeezed it, and removed it from her leg. Letting it plop on Wiley's tray.

He grabbed his plastic cup. "I've done everything to make this a nice getaway, Luanne."

She gathered her just below shoulder length amber hair. Trip marveled at how it dangled and bounced just so on her delicate shoulders, and tied it in a ponytail. Folding her arms, she shut her eyes. "We'll see," she said.

Those were the last words she spoke until the jetliner's pilot got on the intercom to announce they were arriving at their final destination. The jetliner banked, landing gear whirred, and the cabin pressure made their ears pop as they descended upon the Florida Peninsula. Something in the pilot's universal good old boy tone, about remaining seated until they reached the terminal sent a shiver through Trip Wiley. He didn't let his mind linger long, because Luanne's eyes "as blue as the sky" were staring at him, and her hand now clutched his. "Are we here?" She hated air travel. Trip knew, but there was something else in her eyes, something beyond fear of flying, that struck him. Some obscure ideation that this might very well be the final destination.

Moments later they touched down at Miami International airport. A man in a chauffeur's uniform was among the crowd of awaiting arrivals, with a placard that had the word: "WILEY" on it in bold letters.

* * *

45

PHARMACY

The bells above the drug store's door jingled as it was pulled open against the resistance of an old hinge. A whoosh of hot air crept in, lingered a bit, and dissipated in the icy air of the towns sole pharmacy.

It was wedged between a dry-cleaner and Chinese takeout on the right hand side of a busy street. The pharmacy was a multipurpose dwelling that sold a host of curios, candies, and sodas at double the price. In a town overlooked by the big chains.

The pharmacist at the back of the store wore a light blue smock, held a package up to the light, squinted, and pushed his wire framed glasses up his nose. He shook his head with the authority of an owner—as the sign next to the prescription counter confirmed, and effortlessly glanced up. Probably someone in for a pack of smokes, maybe a soda.

He could put two and two together fast, and in an avuncular tone: either fill your prescription, or toss your ass out on a whim, his whim. Doug Ellspie, Registered Pharmacist, had owned Ellspies Pharmacy in Yaptahatchee Springs for twenty-nine years. Before that, his father. He was accustomed to the towns regulars, filling prescriptions from the handful of old-timer docs or dentists. As well as a few well heeled city slickers, who ventured out this way to sightsee a bit before or after their doctor's appointment. The outpatient medical center just went up, with its highfalutin doctors from the big city hospital, and its research facility.

Sure, Ships Clinic brought jobs to the town, but it also brought undesirables, and among those undesirables were the drug seekers. Folks who'd come in with curious looking prescriptions for some dope. Lots of folks had the cancer, and plenty folk had sleep troubles. But kids coming' in for a big quantity of narcotics? Nope. Not in Doug's fine family pharmacy. Not today, not tomorrow, not ever. Doug Ellspie was fully prepared to say no, and if push came to shove, his "peacemaker," occupied an easy to reach spot next to his cash register. "Dopers," Doug would tell his staff, all two of them, Grandma Wilbert, and little Mary Anne. "There's no place for drugs in a drug store." Neither of them understood exactly what he meant, and remained satisfied stocking the store with greeting cards, seasonal tchotchkes, overpriced gift wrapping, ribbons, and bows.

Their major points of contention concerned the sunglasses rack, which didn't seem to be a big seller. Doug knew that, but since it was at the end of the over-the-counter bowel medicines, condoms, and home yeast infection products, didn't care to move it. For gosh sakes folks needed a little privacy. Grandma W and Mary Anne didn't argue, and fancied themselves looking busy. Doug was always restocking the shelves with cheap Chinese keychains, postcards displaying bikini clad gals, muscle boys, and of course, the photo op pictures of Yaptahatchees main draw: Airboat tours, fishin', and gator hunts. In fact, there were blow up water toys in the shape of swamp gators for sale. Big balloon-like water toys that no sane parent would permit little Timmy to float on in the swamp, but may take home to frolic with. Easy profit. Doug had a "deal" with the Chinese restaurant slash entrepreneur next door.

There were all sorts of home health care goods scattered throughout the store: Port-A-Potty, walkers, canes, bandages, lotions and potions. All sorts of remedies marked up for the tourist's headaches, toothaches, diarrhea, tummy aches, or whatever ailed them. Short of what he kept under lock and key behind the pharmacy counter. That was off-limits to all but licensed pharmacists, or pharmacy techs. No trouble here. Nope none at all. Doug never had to trifle with dopers like the big city druggists. He had a nice rapport with law enforcement. Only once had to call on a deputy, and that was because of some kids who tried stealing a jug of ten year old soda. He he he. Got that little bugger but good.

He explained the use of a medication to Mrs. White Socks, with how-to apply instructions legible to any twelve year old. The floral dressed woman still didn't get it. She was one among many of the stores regular customers from the trailer park community west of the main drag. Like most Yaptahatcheen's, unlikely to score well on the verbal portion of an SAT test. In fact, they were unlikely to know what SAT stood for, and found their high school diploma more than sufficient to live prosperously in the town they grew up in, and would raise their children in. In fact, there was a picture of the local high school mascot on the wall: You guessed it, a bull gator smoking a corncob pipe.

When the woman finally understood that the eye-drops prescribed by Doc Beaufort be applied twice per day, she grinned apologetically, opened her purse, and handed the pharmacist a twenty dollar bill. He was just counting out her change when the store's bells jingled. Standing at the pharmacy counter was a man dressed unlike his usual fare, holding a prescription pad.

Who the Hell was this fella standing at the counter? The gal with the floral dress was walking away counting her change, satisfied with the fine instructions precisely explained, and bumped into the man. She locked eyes with him briefly, and would later recall this fella didn't come from these parts. No siree. Must be trouble. The pharmacist would agree.

Doug Ellspie looked at the prescription pad and pen in Trip Wiley's hands, and considered the flutter in his gut as a warning: that this might be trouble. Ain't never seen the likes of this fella. Doug glanced at the "Peacemaker," considering briefly this might be some crazed hippie.

* * *

Part 3

SATAN AND EUSTICE GO OUTSIDE.

Eustice heard the crunch of tires on the gravel driveway, and looked out the window. It wasn't Trip Wiley, Eddy, or one of the girls cars. The running lights—designed to increase visibility while moving—were on. Not something real common in these parts. No sense usin' up good battery, Seeney thought, as he watched the sleek car pull around the circular drive and come to a stop. He just stared at it, half wondering if he should go out and say hello, or wait and see who it was. Eustice looked at his Louisville Slugger, but knew that it wouldn't make much defense against any weapon someone in a car that fancy drove. It sat there and idled, more like purred. Unlike most of the vehicles that'd made their way up the cul-de-sac, puttering on down the lane. Mufflers poked or rusted through. His "guests," had rental cars from the Ft Lauderdale Airport. But they were all milk toast, no nonsense rides that struck the utilitarian jugular.

A cop'd be hard pressed to figure Trip or anyone with a rental—even though they were who they were—as anything but tourists. It wasn't from around these parts either, which were mostly utility vans, pickup trucks, or SUV's. All of them, at least to Seeney's recollection, equipped with a trailer hitch, and usually some sort of craft in tow. Hell this was Yaptahatchee County, and pert near everyone had a rig `tached so they could toss a line in the crick, or unload an airboat. To skedaddle on into the county's main attraction, the swamp, its tributaries, on into Lake Okeechobee, and fish.

Ain't no way this fancy ride had no trailer hitch. Seeney knew—but didn't know exactly how he knew it—just who it was behind the wheel. He stared out the window and waited. He would later swear there was no telling what the driver was doing, or if he was just going to sit there. There was no way of telling if the motor'd been stopped, until he saw the running lights shut off.

The car was a black Audi A8 with tinted windows. Sleek, elegant, and Seeney would recall from a movie he'd seen, as a later version of a real slick operator's car. His heart felt like a mule kicked him from the inside a few times as he waited. Where the Hell was everyone? Damn. The minutes tiptoed by, like they had baby elephants on their backs. Finally he saw the top of a man's head. A big shock of white hair rose above the driver's side door. He seemed to press hard against a resistant door hinge. That was unusual, because fancy cars were greased for easy entry and exit.

This fella had to be in a bad way. Yep, had to be. He watched as a man with very gray, iron like skin, in a dark suit, came walking very slowly, one foot in front of the other around the car's hood and front end. Shee-yatt, the fella was dressed like an undertaker! He took a piece of paper out of his jacket pocket, looked at it, then tossed it onto the stones. Eustice saw it burst into a tiny flame, then a billow of smoke raised. "Shee-yatt!" Seeney leaned back against the wall and took a few deep breaths.

"I ain't scared'a you sumbitch, uh-uh," he repeated six or seven times. By then he gathered himself, to respond to the first of a series of faint knocks at his front door.

Eustice pushed himself away from the wall, and righted himself the best he could. Ran a hand down the front of his work shirt—powder blue and frayed—and hitched his left hand in his jeans pocket.

"Who is it?" Eustice's voice cracked. Collsarnit. Sound like a damn candy-ass chicken shit. Get it together Eustice, get it together.

"You know perfectly well who it is Seeney. Open the door."

Eustice unlocked all three security bolts and slowly pulled the door open an inch and peeked out.

"Are you who I think you are?"

"Shut up Seeney, and get me a drink. Bourbon will work. No rocks."

"Well I'll be . . ."

"Don't even say it." The man said. His voice was strained, like he was pushing air from his lungs, past chunks, or gooey gobs of snot, or who knows . . .tumors?

"I ain't sayin' but for nothin'."

"Good. Fix one for yourself." The man said.

"Oh yes Seeney, I did tell you about those chips. Where are they?"

"Collsarn Nacho Cheese Doritos? Hell's a poppin', Satan. You leave you're manners in Hades?"

"Sifer you dolt! My name, here on this forsaken planet, in this plane of reality is, Lewis Sifer. Don't slip up on that again, or I'll have to—"

"Have to what you dummy? Ain't nothin' you can do to me ain't already been done. I ain't damned no more, and you know it Satan. That's right Satan! I'll call you whatever I plum feel like callin' you. Get it? You still want those chips, huh?" Eustice didn't wait for a reply. "Just keep your collsarn demonical, bull-pucky, to yourself."

The gray man was still standing next to the front door. He watched Eustice go off toward what must have been his kitchen, and heard him open and shut a few cabinets loudly. There was a rattle of glass, and the chug chug chug sound of liquid pouring. He stared at the framed velvet Jesus picture, a collector's edition of American Flag plates, and an array of stuffed alligator heads adorning the walls, and cleared his throat.

"I'm comin', I'm comin', just hold your horses."

"Take your time and hurry up. I don't have an eternity."

Eustice brought out a bottle of Wild Turkey and two glasses. Filled one about three fingers and handed it to the gray man. He watched the old fellow swallow it in a gulp, and hold out the glass for a refill, which he downed just as quickly.

"Whoa, whoa, whoa cowboy, I don't want you throwin' up on my good furniture."

The gray man looked at the glass, it had a Miami Dolphins logo on it, and shook his head. Then scanned the room looking for what Eustice thought was a place to sit down.

"This is how you pissed away the money you got from your settlements?"

"Hey, this is some fine stuff." Eustice replied.

"Please. What is this 'Early Kmart?'" Satan said gruffly, belched, and sat down in a Barcalounger with a thump. Sending a billow of air out like whoopee cushion.

"Hey you're in my favorite chair!"

"That's too bad Seeney. It's where I choose to sit, and I am your guest, right?"

"You may be a guest, but that welcome mat don't say help yourself to bein' a collsarn asshole." Eustice took the unopened bag of corn chips and set them on the coffee table next to a stack of magazines.

Satan held up the bag of chips, ripped it open with his teeth, and looked at the stack of magazines. "Bass Fisherman? Please."

"Please what?"

"You really are one of earth's little bumpkins, aren't you. That's not a question. After all you have seen this is what you elect to do with your life? Ha."

"Ha to you Mr. Mephistopheles." Eustice sat down on the sofa facing the gray man. The television was to his right, Satan's left, and the screen was dark. "You want me to put on the TV? Or you wanna tell me what you got in mind for this trip to earth?"

"In due time. I need a few things to keep this body working."

"I reckon that's why you left a message for me to get you some drugs and whores. You're really fittin' in here, Satan."

"Sifer. Lewis Sifer. I am paying for this."

"Hey Lewis, or maybe I ought call you by some real crummy name, like doody head, huh?"

"Please, you insolent cretin."

"Watch who you're callin' a creature."

"Cretin," the man said. "An impudent, impertinent, brazen, malapert, rude, shameless hick, is what you are Seeney. No more, no less. A cretin is merely a mindless member of mankind. A genetic flaw from your creators little bag of defects. However the analogy—you do understand the meaning of that—a similarity as such, perhaps a comparison of another. Nonetheless, equally brainless in their dealings."

"Shut on up Satan. You're in mah home, and that sorta language can get you a real cattywompin'."

At that the phone rang.

Eustice didn't move. Both of them stared at the telephone.

"Answer it," Satan said.

"It'll go right to voicemail."

"Answer the damn phone Seeney."

"All right all right, I got it. Go on fix yourself another drink."

The gray man was pouring from the bottle, as Seeney lifted the phone up and put his finger to his lips. "It's Doc Wiley. I gotta go check somethin' you just make yourself at home—uh, well you know—eat some chips while I go fetch somethin'."

"Who was that?" Lewis Sifer asked.

"Who was who?"

"The phone you imbecile. The telephone."

"Doc Wiley's on the way."

"Good. Have him pick up some things for me." Satan removed a slip of paper from his pocket and gave it to Eustice.

Seeney stared at it, and shook his head. "Ain't but one drug store in town. I don't know if they got all this stuff."

"They'll have it." Satan said, in a tone resonating so firmly it shook the walls of the rig.

"Okey dokey Satan, iffen ya'all say so. I'll call him back now." Eustice said.

Lewis Sifer went to work on the booze, and began shoveling chips into his mouth.

6 6 6

46

BACK TO THE PHARMACY

Eustice's House

Satan was talkin' out loud, drunk, and stupid soundin', not payin' nary a mind to me. I had a shovel in my hands, and knew I had me but one chance and took it.

I bopped Satan's raggedy ass body but good, whilst he was nit pickin' about my stuffed gator collection. Yep, Ole Mister Mephistopheles himself in some drug addicted, alcoholic, diabetic—and from what Doc Wiley said, cancer ridden body. Hell I got to thinkin' this tweren't even his own body for cryin' out loud. It was however, somebody else's. I had to reckon, if Satan hadn't whirled and twirled into it like a tornadic cyclone it'd be deader than a bucket of rocks. Yeah I cattywomped him, had to. That there was the only way I could do what I'd had in store for him. He done already gathered up all the poop on life's crumminess, and I reckoned that was enough to keep his sorry Satanic ass down Hades way, for another millennium. Ain't no reason to keep him here on earth.

He done got to sex up hookers, shot heroin, pop Oxys, drink all my good liquor up, and smoke more cigs than Winston Salem makes in a year. Then again he was smokin' reefer too, and sniffin' cocaine as well. Hellfire, if Satan wasn't the Devil Himself I'd have to reckon he'd go straight to Hell. So I took the liberty I'd had, right there in my own backyard overlookin' the `Glades, my airboat, and all the critters out there. I knew Satan didn't have no power over the sea beasts, and had to figure the Everglades was part of that Kingdom Phylum Species shebang, and they'd make hay with that already dead body Satan was livin' in. I'd show the Devil just what sufferin' is all about.

I had to think for a spell if he was really livin', or if this thing Satan'd been inhabitin' was a zombie. I laid down the shovel I done whomped him with, and set down to catch my breath, when I heard the sirens. Shee-yatt! How'n tarnation'd the cops get wind of what was goin' on down here? Don't ask how I knew they was comin' for me, I just knew it. I jumped on up and dragged Lucifer by his ankles to my airboat.

Lemme tell you somethin' about airboats. Most folks think they's all the same. No siree. I got me a custom made rig, and some'd say that my rig's the Cadillac of airboats. First a bit about `em: The engine and propeller are inside of an enclosed protective metal cage. That prevents stuff on the outside like trees, tree limbs, branches, folks clothin', beer containers, passengers, or wildlife from gettin' all chopped up in the big ass whirlin' propeller. That collsarn thing'd take a fellas arm right off.

ME AND MR. MEPHISTOPHELES

Hoowee. I seen some devastatin' damage to folks, and also seen the vessel get wrecked too. There's been folks got traumatic injuries so bad they look like they been through a meat grinder. And bein' an operator, takin' passengers on tours as a youngen, I had to be right in tune with my vessel. The propeller's driven by a big ass car engine, or sometimes an airplane motor, and it produces a rearward column of air that propels the collsarn airboat forward.

You steer it with the joystick and some pedals, that make the rudder go this or that way, dependin' on where you're goin'. It's accomplished by forcin' air to be passin' across vertical rudders. There's gotta be a right forceful airflow in order for the vessel to be steered. Airboats don't have brakes. Hoowee is that important. Hellfire I remember when I was just startin' out, I plum ran one up on a sand bar and got stuck there for pert near a weekend. Lucky for me I had me plenty of brews, and carton of Pall Malls, but that there was a few lifetimes ago.

Airboats are incapable of travelin' in reverse. So you best know where you're goin', or there's no end to where you might end up. Another useful factoid for you unindoctrinated. Then there's this: unless the prop design is collective pitch, you can just go on forever. Stoppin' and changin' direction are independent from each other, and based on the operator—a guy like me— also known to you unprofessionals, as a pilot or driver, whatever you wanna call the man on the stick, he is the boss.

I was always Top Gun at the driver's position when takin' folks on tours. The passengers sit in elevated seats, that allows `em to see over the terrain, mostly the swamp vegetation, gators, and all that nature. The visibility depends on how high you stack up the seats. I'd rack `em high for a spell, till some kid pert fell right off. Good thing I rescued the little fella. Still had all his fingers and toes. Maybe didn't walk right for a spell, but hey, that's the business. The Glades ain't no walk in the park. Keepin' the passengers outta the way permits the operator to observe pert near everything in an airboat's path.

Airboat's is all flat-bottomed designed, and there are no operatin' parts below the waterline. Wouldn't want to chop up nothin' in a US Forest Service Preserved area, that'd be a hefty fine. That also lets the vessel be navigated easily, through the shallows in swamps, on in through marshes, into tiny canals, into rivers if you gotta bust a move, and then out onto a lake. Hell, you can even run a nice aluminum hull over the ice on a frozen lake if you wanted. I knew a fella on the lam who'd skedaddled across Lake Erie from Cleveland to some Canuck City.

Nope, ain't nothin' finer than a good runnin' airboat with a top notch engine. The airboat's design makes it the ideal vessel for savin' folks too. Say there's a flood or a hurricane, and they need you to take to rescuin' stranded folks. I used to pick up some nice money workin' for the Coast Guard after one storm or another. But that's a whole different story too.

ME AND MR. MEPHISTOPHELES

Steering an airboat ain't easy. I had to keep that in mind, to do what I was about to. I heard them sirens gettin' closer, and wasn't sure if this was gonna be possible. In light of what needed to be done, and what could be done.

You see, steerin' an airboat is accomplished by swivelin' them vertical rudders positioned at the rear of the vessel. They call it the stem, don't ask me why. On account it don't look like no flower. The big ole propeller produces a column of air so forceful, that it produces a forward momentum. That column of air passes across the rudders like a dozen elephants fartin' at once, like they done just et a ton of refried beans. That gush of breeze is directed through the forward and backward movement of a vertical stick located on the operator's left side. The "stick" is attached to the rudders via teleflex cable, and a kit and caboodle of linked rods. So the overall steerin' and control is: dependin' on the water current, how deep the water is, the wind, and that big ole propeller's thrust.

I heard the sirens stop. That meant John Q. was near, maybe already up front. I had to move, but they might hear me. I yanked hard, pullin' Satan's feet, loadin' him on board. I jumped in to start `er on up.

The sound made by an airboat's propeller and engine can be real loud, mine sure's Hell was. Most of the sound is produced by the propeller. Modern airboat designs, like mine, use the top of the line technology, and got significantly reduced sounds.

Unless you wanna switch it out and make a ruckus. Most modern airboat engines are equipped with mufflers. Mine was `cause I liked sneakin' up on nude sunbathers. Multi-blade, carbon-fiber propellers really cut down on the sound comin' from an airboat. Oh yeah, if you didn't know: Airboats vary in size from standard 10-foot long hunt trail boats with a two-to three-passenger capacity, to the large eighteen-passenger, and way bigger tour boats.

I had me a custom, someplace in the middle sized craft. And already had Satan strapped to the bow. We was maybe fifty yards into the swamp when I heard the first cop's voice comin' out all cackley from a bullhorn:

"Shut down the engine and return to shore. Step away from the airboat and put your hands in the air!" Vroom said my rig. Vroom vroom vroom.

* * *

184

47

I was expectin' to hear the Coast Guard Chopper's whomp, whomp, whomp, zonin' in on me. I waited a sec or two, looked around, and didn't see but for nothin'. I tweren't sure what was goin' on, because as crooked as lots of lawmen are, not all of `em fall under Satan's spell. Iffen this was a real shake down there'd be a whole lot more than a few fellas on shore. Nothin'. I could hear the distant whap whap whappin' of the chopper, and the siren sounds far away. Whatever it was they were doin' didn't have but for nothin' to do with me, here now. Just me and Satan.

I wasn't sure if the real cops—not Lucifer's minions—was really after me, and I tweren't gonna push no envelopes. Nope. Whatever was gonna happen out here in the swamp was between me and whatever lie ahead. No outsiders, and no law. I didn't have no trouble with the law these days, so maybe they wasn't really cops at all.

I just throttled up my rig and headed toward the thickest mangroves I knew. I waited till I made a few zigs and zags around a clump of sawgrass, or patch of mangrove, before assessing' my situation. I wasn't right sure if what I thought was real. Or some idea Satan or one of his minions tweaked in my head to look after their demon boss? I had to know.

Lookin' behind my rig at the wake of my airboat, the folks on shore didn't fit the bill of any shakedown I'd ever seen. I been in `em, and real cops don't go trampling' on personal property without a warrant. Due process they call it. I knew that much. And sure's Heck there wasn't no probable cause for nothin'. I throttled back a might and looked over at Mr. Mephistopheles. I reckon if John Q Law saw a fancy dressed geezer all hogtied like my guest here, they might get to askin' some questions. But then I had to wonder what sort of mischief his body'd been up to on his way on up from Hades, through America, and on over to my front door. I did let the Devil in, and like the old saying goes: "When the Devil's at your door, and you let him in. . ." Somethin' like that. Blah blah blah, I had the Prince of Darkness tied up just fine in my airboat, and he was about to get a taste of earth's finest sufferin' of the flesh available.

I ain't no torturing sadistical fella, but . . .

Lookin' over at Satan all helpless, I can't say I didn't have me no reservations. We're not talkin' Denny's here, we're talkin' high end Mu-shu water-boarding, worst pain you can inflict on a human stuff.

ME AND MR. MEPHISTOPHELES

I gotta tell you that even though this was the Devil himself, I didn't feel right in that pang of conscience sort of way. A fella who'd been to Hell, who'd been a rabble rouser, ought to feel—given the chance—to sock it to the worst critter in all creation. Maybe it was the suit. I got to thinkin', if he was stripped down to the gray, ghoulish, birthday suit he'd stole from that soon to be dead, disease ridden body, what I was about to do'd be easier. Yep. That's the plan I fixed in my head.

I checked the twine I tied him up with, and gave it a yank. I think he may have groaned, kicked him good in the head with my boot heel a couple times to make sure he was still out, and aimed my craft toward where I'd arranged to meet with the Doc, and whoever he was bringin' to finish this up.

I hope Doc Wiley's GPS doohickey was workin', and all went well with what we had in store for this crumb. But I also knew these waters, and as dark came closer even the best plans can go kablooey. The deeper into the wild we went more and more questions popped up in my head. Questions I ought considered before agreeing' to help Satan make Hell more Hellish.

Collsarnit! There had to be a Hell. That there is a fact. There'd be absolute chaos in the corporeal world if all of a sudden the Hell they may've thought they were goin' to just stopped being, right? I knew that Hell. It was a crummy place, and bad as it was, imaginatin' a universe without it? Hell no.

At that very moment when I was imaginatin', my boat started rockin'. I thought it was maybe some rocks or a sand bar. Maybe I run up on some weeds. But the rockin' got somethin' fierce, and the airboat—I swear I ain't never seen or felt nothing' like it—started spinning' around like I was in some big ole toilet, and a giant just hit the flush handle. Hellfire! I was in some swirling vortex that sped up round and round so fast I got dizzy. I felt an urge to puke, but held it in. The waves around the boat were sloshin' up, comin' in over the aluminum hull, soakin' Satan to the skin. My feet was drenched. I swear the boat was goin' under, and I didn't wanna be no gator food. I heard the engine sputter, gasp, and drown out. Damn thing was flooded. Damn damn damn. I raised my hand up to the sky. Curse this whole shebang! How could I let myself be a pawn in this cosmic game. How could I let myself be duped into aiding and abetting the worstest of the worst. I felt the most awful I'd ever felt, even in my darkest times of death, dyin', and losin' all I'd had. What was my life all about? Why why why? I remember a rush of blood fillin' my head like I was maybe gonna pass out, and I fell to my knees. I don't right know what happened next, but it was as if the earth shifted somehow. The boat wasn't movin' and all nature stopped. The birds quit chirpin, the wind died out, and a stillness came over the swamp like all time stopped. I looked up, and out of no-place a big ole cloud's over me, and then another, and another. What the Hell? I stood up, cupped my hands over my eyes and looked all around.

Nothin'. Maybe it'd rain. What'd been a clear afternoon looked like rows of dark clouds linin' up at the starting gate at a Nascar Race. Then lightnin' the color of fancy bar lights, and thicker than a fat lady's big belly started zig-zaggin' across the sky. They were pink, and orange, and that pukey lime green color of mental hospitals, only bright like fireworks. Then pink neon that could've spelled out the name of my favorite beer set to doin' a dance that looked hotter than a humongous blowtorch. The lightning bolts jumped from one black cloud to another like they were doin' a sparkly dance. Looked like mental folks havin' cosmic spasms.

Faster and faster and then there was a sound so loud it knocked me on my ass. Shee-yatt! I think I passed out for a few seconds. I couldn't see but for nothin', and started rubbin' my eyes. I rubbed so hard tears was rollin' down my cheek. I could just make out a blurry gob of who knows what. Shaped like people, two of `em bathed in the same bright mishmash of fireworks and molten light I'd seen in the sky. I don't know how long it lasted, or what it was, but remember sittin' on my rump next to Satan, lookin' up at two beings. Gradually goin' from critters of light into human type people. My eye focus started comin' back and like nothin' outside of a dream, or a bad drug trip, there was two people standin' there on my airboat sure as the day is long. A man and a woman. A colored guy, and not-so-bad lookin' gal. At first I was too shocked to do but for nothin', but in the blink of a corpuscle that all changed.

48

In my mind's deepest cavities, deeper than the ones in my teeth, I knew who they was. I had dealin's with `em in the past. And they cast a glow of good vibes like that feelin' you get when you take a pee.

Holy shee-yatt. Satan had an expression like he was gonna bust a gut, and when he saw these apparitions went into thrashin' like a bull gator caught in a net. Nope they weren't his minions. No siree. If you ever saw a person go white from fear, Ole Mr. Mephistopheles's color made that look like he'd not only seen a ghost, but two of `em, who'd just spray painted him with White-Out!

Maybe it was far worse for Ole Mister Mephisto `cause he went wrigglin' and jigglin' somethin' fierce, chantin' some echo sounds, like he was summoning' his minions.

Somethin' was funny, not in that ha ha funny way. Actually it was all sorta off-kilter in a not so earthly way. Like that misty fog you have, when you wake up from a crummy dream. I'd been transported. How was anyone gonna find me, and if they did would it matter? Was I dead again?

"No Eustice you aren't dead." It was the woman, Ellen K. Hall. She read my mind. I knew it, I collsarn knew it.

"She's right, Mon." The big guy said.

I looked up at these folks and actually smiled. I couldn't believe it myself. The colored guy with the Rasta Dreadlocks offered me a hand to get back on my feet, and the gal spoke in a voice that sounded like sandpaper dragged over silk sheets.

"Hello Eustice," she held out a Highball glass of who knew what. I drank it right quick.

"We're here to help with the rubbish Mon," the colored guy said. He looked down at Satan, who was chantin', and squirmin' fiercer and fiercer.

"I reckon you might say I got me a few answers about right and wrong," Eustice said. By way of a visit from my guardian angels. I felt a wash of somethin' come over me like a waterfall, and shut my eyes. Then a starburst of all the ideas and thoughts I ever had filled my head.

It was what I gotta say the absolutist best burst of happiness a human could have. I ain't never felt so comforted. And it lasted for a spell. This beat any drug, booze, sexin', or anything. I don't right know how long it lasted, and didn't care. I wanted it to last forever, but it passed. I knew deep down inside that everything was gonna be okay . . . Or was it? Something changed.

I looked over at where Satan was hogtied and nearly shit a peanut. That sumbitch was gone!

* * *

49

TRIP IS TRIPPED UP

I had a feeling about this bumfuck drug store, in the middle of swamp dweller, trailer park country, but went in anyway. The place had that cloyingly sweet smell of a dental office with the addition of rotting candy, and old and very useless sundries. Sunscreen that was so past its expiration date it would burn flesh. The postcards could have been snapshots of a trip to the 1950s, and the suntanned people on the cards were probably in nursing homes or dead by now. The not-so-cute Confederate Flags positioned around the shop made me uneasy, as did the weary glare of the stores workers. They had that look of simple country folk, whose narrow gazed stares sized me up, catalogued, and decided I'd best get on with what I was doing or else. The pharmacist had glanced over at me when I first walked in, and went on with doing his thing. I was a passerby whose business they could've done without.

This was their neck of the woods, and I'd best be careful how I act, or what I say. I had a sense that accidents could happen in these parts, and the gals behind the counter had the look they could be arranged. After all, this was the Glades, and people have been known to disappear out here never to seen from again.

Oddly the hustle and bustle of Miami, Fort Lauderdale, and all the urban decay of the last few decades was only a few miles away. History seemed to have skipped over this bubble. Things have remained unchanged in these parts since World War II.

I was expecting some singsong, good old hyper-countrified cordiality, but it didn't come. The clerks just looked at me the way a vulture might view road kill. Come on down! Yeah, right.

"Help you?" Said the older woman behind the counter to my left. There were rows of cigarette boxes, and a younger woman beside her, who smiled falsely. She looked like someone who'd never sat in a dental chair.

"I need the pharmacy," I said.

"On back," the older woman said.

I walked down the aisle in the shadow of Neon light toward the pharmacy. I feared no evil. I feared idiocy, and backwoods meanness.

ME AND MR. MEPHISTOPHELES

These were prisoners stuck in an era that somehow avoided, evaded, and took pride in its resolute, rebellious reluctance, to recall the Civil War was long past. Maybe nobody told these folks their side lost.

Maybe it was me, but the eyes gazing down at me from the picture of the President of the Confederacy, Jefferson Davis, on the wall reminded me that some wars never end.

I knew where I was and that gave me an inkling of where this could lead. I wasn't in the mood for a trip to Andersonville, and the ghosts haunting that prison for Yankee soldiers. I had enough things to deal with, and surrendered to the task at hand. Cleared my throat and said: "Thanks," and forged on.

* * *

50

POWERS WHO MIGHT BE

Harold Spooky Pollack III died years ago. The woman, Ellen K. Hall, way before that. But here they were with me. I met `em before, on account both of them was already dead. In fact, they worked for The Powers That Be. Ellen was a real elegant lady, all dolled up like an old time movie star. Long sexy hair, fancy dress, cigarette holder, and a glass of booze. The colored fella, Spooky, was as big as pro football player. Wearin' one of them Dashiki Afro shirts, a doobie danglin' from his lip, badass shades lowered down his nose, and balled up fists on his hips. The lady set herself down on the passenger bench lookin' like she was posin' for a photo op. I knew better on account they don't send these folks down from—you know up there—unless there's some real disturbated stuff down here on earth. And with that big ruckus and firework display it looked like the universe was a collsarn pinball machine goin' kablooey.

I knew right then I didn't handle Satan the way I should. Because if phantoms had moods—maybe I best not call `em phantoms—angels, yep angels. If they had moods they wasn't in a real good one. I was eyeballin' Spooky, whom I ain't seen for a spell, and then the pretty dead lady Ellen, when it occurred to me I'd been transported. It hit me like case of the shits after bad sushi. I must've fouled up tryin' to reckon with Satan on my own. Oops.

"Oops is right, Mon." Spooky said. "You do know that the balance of the universe is off."

"What the hay-ell?" I said, scratchin' mah head.

* * *

51

All was still where we was. And don't ask me where that place could be found. Tweren't no GPS that'd locate us, no way, no how. I knew where we wasn't, and it sure's the day is long, not on the good green earth. I done been swept up to some ethereal plane to have some sort of whoop-ti-do with The Power That Be. And was reckonin': if they sent guardian angels along it wasn't gonna be no pep talk. I got to thinkin' I may have put the kibosh on some grand plan, or maybe, just maybe, I was on to somethin' good. I figured I already done the evil stuff, so what was there in between?

I don't right know what's up or what'd down. I stared into the muddy water, and didn't see but nothin'. Did a gator chomp down on one of Ole Mister Mephistos arms or legs, haul him on down under to feed on later? I set there on my airboat, with a toothpick in my mouth wonderin' where zactly I was.

Ain't never been in this part of the swamp. Never knew it existed. Maybe I was tricked.

"No Mon. You ain't been tricked." Spooky said.

"Have a drink sweetheart." The lady said.

"Where'd Satan go?" I asked the colored fella.

"For now, he is simmering down."

"The gators are gonna get to nibblin' at him you know?" I said.

"Yes, Mon. Maybe easier than us strippin away the body."

"What?" Eustice said.

"We need to have a talk with Satan," Ellen said. "Outside of the corporeal body he's been using."

"Yes, Mon. He's had it long enough. He was only given seven days."

"I know I know, he gotta make Hell more Hellish, with ideas he got from visitin' us earth dwellers."

"Do you think he has?" Ellen notched her chin at the water's surface.

"I don't right know," I said. There was some bubbles formin' and a few ripples.

"Mon, I think that he needs to return to Hades with the very knowledge and sensations a human body can have."

"What about the fella whose body he took?" I asked.

"He died a week ago sugar," Ellen said.

"The body was riddled with cancer, drug addiction, pain and misery." Spooky swept his long dark hand. "Bibbidi-Bobbidi-Boo, Satan's grand trickery."

"Spooky," Ellen said, "I think you should add Satan's old favorites: despair, desolation, and a hefty dose of depravity."

"Yes, yes yes. The human condition. You did leave off Lucifer's very own favorite Ellen." Spooky's Rasta accent was replaced with some indiscernible one—at least to Eustice—who just stared at the water's surface.

"I did, didn't I?" Ellen said. "Desire. Ah desire, temptation, and all the things that have driven m—"

"And women." Spooky added.

"Quite right Spooky, quite right indeed. Driven mankind to the brink before time was even measured." Ellen added.

"Them bubbles is gettin' fizzier, and there's some action goin' on under that quilt of water coverin' him."

"Yes there is. Satan's flesh is being stripped from him as we speak." Spooky said.

"Shee-yatt that's gotta be the most painful thing a human could have done to `em."

"We know Eustice. We know." Ellen said.

"So what exactly did you need me for if you was just gonna have him et by gators? Why didn't you just do this in the first place?"

"Eustice," Ellen said, "The Powers That Be forbid us from tampering with corporeal matter."

"We can't touch humans in the sense that an act would occur, or perhaps be registered by your sensory systems. But we can make you feel joyous. As Satan can invoke fear and horror, and lead one to temptation." Ellen held up her glass. "Cheers to being a spirit." She said.

"So I done been used?"

"What Eustice? Did you think after all you've been through, that this universe is fair sweetheart?" She tossed back her head, her hair flowing radiantly, as if bathed in light. Eustice would later recall.

"Are you sayin' you got me to do all this?" Eustice looked at the water's surface. "Look at that, looks like it's comin' to a boil."

"The critters are rippin' him apart, and I done kilt a fella when I was in that moment, or whatever you Powers That Be call it. Hellfire I'm a collsarn killer now. I'm gonna go right back to Hell!"

"No. It doesn't work that way." Spooky placed a hand on Seeney's shoulder. "It will be fine Eustice."

"Did I kill someone?"

"No Eustice, you can't kill someone who's already dead." Ellen said.

"Satan's on his way back to Hades, with enough knowledge of the corporeal world to last eons. Hell will remain as it has for a long, long, time."

"And Heaven? Zat still gonna be okay?"

"You might say that you saved our jobs too." Ellen said.

"Yes Eustice, we won't be evaporating into the abyss. Balance is restored, and the alien beings would have surely disposed of us." Ellen said.

"So I reckon I get some credit for all this cosmic good I done, right?" At that moment a lightning bolt struck Eustice, sending him to his knees. Dazed, he fell flat on his face.

* * *

52

SEENEY GOES INTO A THINK

I woke up sittin' in the driver's seat of my airboat. Whatever happened had passed. Somehow I lost consciousness, and righted myself. Maybe them "visitors" did it, set me right. My memory ain't been tampered with on account I recalled it all right clear. Ole Mister Mephistopheles was gnawed alive. Was he ever really livin'? Hell was Hell again, and Heaven was in its place. I pondered that. It just seemed too easy. The angels came and left after all that gigantic cosmic business.

It was supposed to be done. I just wasn't sure. It all happened so quick: me, Satan, Trip, Ellen, Spooky, comin' on in and squarin' things up. I had to think on this. My left hand was on the stick, and there was holes in my thinker brain. I knew a few things here and there, but none of the pieces fit in any puzzle. Because there wasn't no puzzle at all.

I couldn't ask myself why, when, or what I was doin' on account there wasn't anything that rhymed with a bunch of busted up memories. Didn't make sense, and it made all the sense in the world at the same time. I reckon I could've spent the rest of my life there out on the swamp. Bein' alive or dead for reasons I don't think I'll even know, didn't right matter. I'd seen somethin' without seein' it. Felt somethin' without feelin' it. As I set there I felt a sense bubblin' up from my innards. That all of everything should fit into some place just so, right?

I didn't know what time it was. Don't right know if it mattered but looked at the sun. An orange ball, nary a quarter way up in the sky. I wasn't sure if it was risin' or settin'. Streaks of glowin' light shot out in all directions through the clouds. They were puffy clouds laced with colors. They were movin' leisurely like majestic masses shaped like continents on planets nobody's ever seen but me. From this vantage point in the middle of the swamp I thought I could see the whole universe. Trillions of molecules movin' along. All tuned up like an orchestra after the Maestro tapped his baton, and some grand symphony played in sounds inaudible to my ears.

So there I was, sittin' in the driver's seat of my airboat, listenin to my air-cooled engine purr like a kitty cat. It'd begun gettin' darker. That big ole 6-cylinder, water cooled, large displacement engine, with 400 horsepower just idlin' there, smack dab in the middle of no place I done ever seen.

ME AND MR. MEPHISTOPHELES

I looked on back at my fan blade and moved the joystick, swivelin' the vertical rudders in the stern—the back to all you non nautical folks, all was well. I revved `er up to see if she was runnin' all right, and sure enough the propeller whooshed on out a collumn of air, that pushed me on toward wherever it was I was goin'. I set my palm back on the stick attached to them rudders, and got me to wonderin' iffen it was all a dream. If all I'd ever been through weren't but for nothin, but imagined. Wishful thinkin.' I'd somehow made the world a better place.

I looked on over at the horizon. The air was still, so the tips of the long plants was froze in a way that made it seem like the world'd stood still. Just me my airboat and all of nature. At a time of day when it's either just before dawn, or just before dusk. Out here on the swamp early mornin' and early night look the same in lots of ways. And iffen you ain't sure, all you gotta do is sit it out and wait. Dark comes and you're lost, day comes, and you ain't. It was like flippin' a coin. If I stayed where I was I'd be in the hands of fate, whatever the heck that was, and there wasn't no way to be sure. The animals aren't talkin'. I shut down the engine and just set there and waited.

Maybe I was imaginatin', but somethin' was off-kilter. It started with one, two, then three bubbles. The water was smooth as a mirror, made outta some fancy material they build jet planes from. Oh it was really somethin' to look at with all the beautiful lights streamin' over it, glowin' like some famous art picture out of a museum.

But them bubbles. What in tarnation were they? A gator breathin'? Nah. I thought for sure whatever lie beneath that blanket of wet glass was either asleep, or plain done dead. But it weren't. Them bubbles went from a few, to a fizzy pop pop poppin'. In all the quietude of nature, the only sound louder than birds and rustlin' branches. And they was at rest on account there wasn't no breeze. It was the water. Somethin' was astir.

And then BOOM—the swamp exploded like a million hurricanes, and a just as many tornados all at once. A twister lookin' cone poked up toward the sky like an upside down mountain, sendin' my airboat spinnin' somethin' fierce!

Collsarnit!

* * *

53

EUSTICE GOES TO SPACE

I knew it then like I knew these waters. There weren't no way Satan'd just get et by gators and croak a human life. The sky turned bright orange. Like an electrical storm shot off all its lightning at once on the inside of a Jack-O-Lantern. No matter what time of day it was didn't make much of a difference at all. Somehow, someway, and from someplace nobody ain't never seen before, I'd swear it was a UFO. Came outta no place. A letter of the alphabet after Z. That much I knew on account I could recite the alphabet backwards real fast. I do that when I get the heebie-jeebies, or John-Q's flashin' lights is behind me pullin' me over for a sobriety test, ZYXWVU. Hellfire and shit on a stick! Whatever it was that'd come upon me now, was not of this earth, the Hell I'd been to, or the Heaven I've seen. I swear on all things you can swear on, this here was a collsarn flyin' saucer! There was some space folk that'd made their way on terra firma, and they was here for a reason.

I didn't see no Air Force jets scramble like in the movies. No whirly twirly, or loo loo loo sound neither, this spacecraft was as quiet as flea's fart. It was bigger than half the sky, and took in the whole upside down mountain itself. Holy shee-yatt! This was the alien rejuvenators of the hereafter. And whatever Satan figured he'd do wasn't up-to-crumb. You know, up to what that devil was s'posed to do. He plum failed!

There was a some ultra-cosmological threshold the Devil couldn't reach, and this was that chariot that them slaves sung about to carry em' on home. This was in my disheveled freaked out estimation, that earth wasn't up to snuff in spookin' itself out. We earthlings was so amped up with horror and terror, violence and cruelty, that even monsters weren't scary no more. We made all the things that'd turn our inside out, outside in. And that primal urgent mode Doc Wiley explained, "that fight or flight thing we all got," has done been tweaked so hard by the last few decades that humans just scared the fear out of terror. Suicide bombers, cancer, fire, bein' eaten alive, anything humans done did do or say, wasn't nothin' compared to what these folks might consider spooky. And there I was in the front row of what'd surely be a change in all humanity forever. Maybe them aliens wanted a witness, or maybe they didn't know or care if a dumb old human was lookin', because they sucked whatever was once Satan himself outta the swamp, and swept him on into their craft. Like my very own vessel: capable of achieving high speeds, and cruise quietly with great ferocity, and then be gone.

ME AND MR. MEPHISTOPHELES

I was stunned. Like I done got me a jolt of Taser bolts shot through me over and over. I had to be movin' on back to find out how to summon them angels back here. Shee-yatt, maybe they done been swept up too! Oh my . . . what do I say? Sweet Jes—that don't work neither. Heaven and Hell in the same place, on the same space ship? My brain pan was leakin' ideas so fast I got dizzy. So dizzy I felt like I was gonna start throwin' up.

Would my rig still be on shore?

I gotta get me a ride on the spaceship. Somethin' was pushin' me, like a fat lady at the deli tryin' to get a gander at the chopped herring.

* * *

54

TRIP WILEY BEATS THE RAP

Doug Ellspie, RPh, narrowed his eyes, cleared his throat, and slipped his unseen fingers around the Colt's grip. He did not intend on filling any of the prescriptions the so-called Doctor had written from his prescription pad and placed on the Lucite counter. "You may not have all of this is, but fill as much as you can." Trip said.

"We don't fill no prescriptions for strangers," Doug Ellspie, RPh said, pointing the business end at Doc Wiley without ceremony. "Put your hands where I can see them, and stay where you are until the law gets here. Granny, Mary, go make the call!" Grandma Wilbert and little Mary Anne looked on at the pharmacist knowing what was going to happen, and acted accordingly.

"You're making a mistake," Trip Wiley said, as he looked at the weapon.

ME AND MR. MEPHISTOPHELES

A Colt Single Action Army—also known as the Model P, Peacemaker, M1873, Single Action Army, SAA, and the Colt .45, was pointed just below Trip Wiley's left eye.

"Shut the hell up, weirdo." Doug said, and cocked the gun.

Trip heard the weapons mechanism as the chamber spun and the gun's hammer pulled back. Shit, this asshole meant business. Must be the sideburns. Fucking mutton chops and mop of hair did seem out of place, or so Luanne said.

She was noshing on the remains of a bag of Nacho Cheese Doritos, when Trip pulled the rental into a parking space in front of the drug store. He told her to wait while he filled some prescriptions for Satan. Damn that did come out sounding crazy, as if he gave it time to sink in. But the Devil was at Seeney's, and keeping him at some steady state was imperative for all to go according to plan. Whatever that was. No, Trip did not make a chart for the rascal, or do much at all to document the myriad of medical anomalies justifying the polypharmacy he was about to collect.

Luanne, the reluctant traveler, knew from her high school days in Akron, and later confirmed at the stripper bar among the pole dancers: that the drugs he was going to score, although legitimate, would be a problem. They certainly couldn't have taken it along on their journey.

How could anyone know what drugs the Devil would need. Hell, some of these Trip had on the list were a flat out a mystery to her. Then again they wouldn't be a mystery to the druggist. She crumpled up the bag, tossed it on the floor, and fished around in her purse for a cigarette.

At the pharmacy counter: Trip saw some tightening of the pharmacists trigger finger, suggesting that it would certainly put an end to his life. Spraying blood, skull chips, and chunks of brain all over the the drugstore. That old hag, Grandma W, and the lovely little Mary Anne, were ready in Wiley's mind. He was fully aware if the wrong words were uttered, or he seized the opportunity to gain store integrity, the general laziness endemic to swamp folk could change instantly. "Why would you want to shoot me?" Trip asked in a cool, even, fearless tone. "I am a duly licensed physician in the state of Florida. Which if you let me I can demonstrate by showing you my identification."

"Lay it on the counter freak." Doug lowered the gun, but Trip still saw the black hole at its tip. The doom hole. That could be the last memory of his life if trigger finger didn't accept Wiley's bona fides.

"They're all current, Mr. Ellspie." Trip said, reading the letters on his Name Tag.

"They better be."

"You just wrote out prescriptions for anti-neoplastics, heavy pain drugs, erectile dysfunction pills, syringes, insulin, stimulants, amphetamine salts, and heartworm medication? Are you throwing a party at a cancer ward, or a kennel? Don't answer me. You're a freak, look at you. Who are you supposed to be Elvis Presley's long lost nephew? No, no, no, these prescriptions are all wrong." He tightened his grip on the pistol and brought it back up to Trip's left eye.

The bells above the entrance of the pharmacy jingled again. The pharmacist looked up for a fraction of a second. Just long enough. Trip calculated in his mind: to pivot, sweep his left arm across the counter, and make contact with the lateral aspect of his wrist, the area just below the short sleeve of his blue smock, the antecubital fossa. Crumpling the grip on the gun with his left hand. He would bring down a punishing blow to the pharmacists clavicle. Maybe snap it, maybe not, but he'd still be conscious. Trip would have a gun on him, and the prescriptions would be filled, plus whatever goodies he might need for himself and Luanne.

Mary Anne and Grandma were looking on, just as Luanne asked for a pack of Newport's. The Colt clattered on the counter, and Trip swooped it up.

"Trip, whatever you're doing you better hurry up." Luanne tapped the tobacco in the pack on her palm, undid the cellophane wrapper, stopped, and stared at the two women, placing a cigarette from the pack in her mouth. "I need a light."

"I won't be long, just go start the car and wait." Wiley stared at the pill counter, and Doug rubbing his broken clavicle. "You didn't have to break it," the pharmacist whimpered.

"You didn't have to be an asshole. Just fill the prescriptions."

A distant siren filled the little shop, that just echoed jolly sleigh-bell greetings.

"The cops will get you Elvis."

"Shut the fuck up and get moving. No tricks. I'll be watching real close."

* * *

55

EUSTICE SEENEY BETWEEN HEAVEN HELL AND WHAT IN THE...

I'm someplace that ain't a place at all, no siree. It's orange and luminous, and I'd swear my thinker brain wasn't connected to nothin'. I was watchin' the universe in all its entirety unfold, and then flop back onto itself. Everything was whirlin' around like the innards of a tornado. Only what I saw made pukin' up anything just a nutty notion, on account everything everywhere was turned inside out!

I saw trees innards spewed all over dog guts, cat guts, gator bits, and all the critters around me a few minutes back was all bein' turned inside out. Like some big ole fist reached down and yanked `em out by their tails. Was I next? Oh my good gracious great whatever I can pray to. I seen strangers I ain't never knew goin' to Heaven or Hell, and they was flyin' around with the critters and plants. There was a wind that tweren't no wind like I ever reckoned, on account whatever was blowin' was in color! How could that be?

Don't think I'll ever know. And them folks I was with: Spooky, Ellen K. Hall, and Satan hisself was in the form of a lump of coal, or big ole pile of doody. They was standin' on some piece of world, or a slice of earth, what was left of it. I knew the planet done been destroyed by The Powers, beyond anything ever known by earthly humans. I looked Satan fair in the beady red bulb eye holes. He was just some clump of evil I ain't ever seen. And somehow the colored guy and pretty gal remained unchanged. They wasn't bein' turned inside out, so there must be some ground rules. I looked down at my feet and nearly shat a bag of peanuts. My feet been turned into bird's legs! Yes siree, chicken's feet. Shee-yatt I has been transmogrified! How did I know what that meant? And I want my feet back now!

There it was, the end or maybe the beginning of everything. Good and evil were but the same in that way stuff's measured. I don't right know if you'd call it mass, weight, or energy.

Doc Wiley'd said weight's and measures came in all sorts of ways: Watts, joules, Coulombs, Svedberg units, Bodanskis, pounds, drams, pints, quarts, ounces, gallons, jugs, meters, miles, kilograms, milligrams, and on and on. Humans was good at measurin' stuff. From time to pie-yoonis size, titties, tools, depths, and pools. Everything in the "known" universe had a time, place, size, and shape. I was now smack dab in a place that was not a place, in the sense places can be found on maps or star charts.

And next to me was some hobgoblin, that wasn't any more evil or good than the other entities on this same plane, if it even was a collsarn plane. No siree, it tweren't no interdimensional zone, it was in a place outside of places. Rhymes, reasons, days, nights, and seasons didn't mean but for nothin' here. But for reasons unknown to me I remained a chicken footed, free-thinkin' critter, in this un-place sort of place. I shut my eyes right hard and hoped maybe I was dreamin'. But what happened was once shut, my eyes was sealed like duct tape been slapped on me hard, fast, and tight enough to seal me in. I couldn't move no more, and my ear drums started to itch. Like they was bein' tickled by fringe. Like someone was playin' the snare drum on my tympanics. Fear had left me like it wasn't part of my being. As if I'd left it on home back at . . . I forgot where home was. And just like that I went into a float. A driftin' puff of air that wasn't air at all. I felt like I was in a jiggly tub of Jello. When would this all end?

* * *

56

Astronomers and physicists at observatories across the globe would scratch their heads wondering how or why a wormhole, in the year 2013, appeared and disappeared, before they could call it a "wormhole." To some it is theoretical: A passage through space and time. It's a shortcut for a long journey across the universe. However, that is not what happened in that fraction of a second that lasted thousands of years. Time stopped relative to who or what was viewing it. And Eustice Seeney was unknowingly at the cusp of one among many micro-tunnels that extended from one point in the universe to another.

Eustice would phrase this as such: "Infinity's a big collsarn place."

"Yes, Eustice, it is." The voice was scratchy, and had a rhythm to it.

Seeney would later recall "Like some hiddidy jibbidy jazz music." "It's too big for my thinker brain to fit the idea of it in. All that jazz is makin' me nuts. I gotta size it up to fit in my head."

"Try this—"

Eustice heard without hearing. Contrary to any known human physiology detailing the "how or why" people hear. Via the tympanic membrane, cochlear vestibular complex, and physiological pathways. No. He heard sans any sound. Rather a non-cellular neurotransmission, kicked into cosmic gear by what no one would dare suggest in the known universe. After all, how could they? This was indeed unknown, unearthly, and so far out of mans capacity to grasp, it had to be taken on faith alone as something beyond. And this is what it was:

"Sounds like some colored fellas are playin' lyrical instruments with non-words. Sayin' stuff that don't fit into pieces of any puzzle, that fits into parts of my head I ain't got. Words that ain't in any dictionary."

"That is correct Eustice," Coltrane said without saying.

"How do you understand me?"

"I am all every." Coltrane said.

"Say what?" I bore down with my mind real hard like I was gonna take a brain dump. Eustice responded.

"Each of your mind's impulses are readable with every surge, you don't need to speak or think. Let yourself go, thoughts will flow. I will understand what's going to be spoken, thought, conceived, before it's considered."

"Who the collsarn . . ."

"Just everything and nothing at the same moment. All moments containing the mass of all that is, and all that is not."

"Damnit Coltrane, you're not makin' no sense."

"Just stand still and let the universe do what it does."

"What in tarnation you talkin' `bout doin' with me. And I want my feet back?"

"I don't know what to do with your species."

"Shee-yatt!" Eustice looked down and had elephant feet and legs. "I want my collsarn feet back!"

"We'll get to that."

* * *

57

GENERAL PRINCIPLE ALONE

An urban legend has circulated the globe for years: When a human dies he's so and so milligrams lighter than when he was alive. They—the legend spreaders—say the soul weighs something, and it leaves your body upon death. Some diet, eh?

Eustice had come to the end of his own beginning. His experience over the course of a decade or so ago. Death on the operating table, and months in a coma brought him to believe wholly: his life prior to that was flawed. He didn't see the "bright white light," rather a "blurry red tunnel," which led to a Hell that may have been of his own device. This happened again, premature demise and a trip to Hell. Followed by yet another death, and trip to Heaven. Heaven wasn't all he expected, and Seeney was revived. In all he'd seen, death and its aftermath, he knew as certainty: as a man there was indeed an afterlife.

However, no one could imagine both Heaven and Hell. Given they believe in either, existed within a greater field of extracorporeal shenanigans, which man has no control over. Nope. Our fate's are signed, sealed, sold, and salvaged by some entity. Eternally recycling the husks of flesh, and reconfiguring the electrical impulses our life force generates. And this is simply the way it is.

So Eustice is tethering in-between what remains of a life well lived—whatever that means—and oneness with the universe. An incorporation into the overall morass of time, space, and eternity. So simple to remain in the grips of a handless, unforgiving, holding pattern, with no runway to land on. A place where choice, freedom, sorrow, humor, pain, and delight are all weighted the same. A nothingness and fullness with no judgement, penalties, vantage points, or horizons. Just stretching on forever in an unforeseeable expanse of an expanding random universe. Nothing binding its parts together as they dissipate into an abyss. Formations of cosmic plateaus folding over and over on to themselves. Seeney pondered these things as he stared down at the elephant stumps that replaced his gator skin boots. He could still miss the simplicity of a stubbed toe, cold beer, and day on the swamp. And he wanted to go back home.

* * *

58

WILEY'S RUMINATIONS

It was nearly an hour past sundown, when I finally was released from custody. A squad car dropped Luanne and me off at my rental unit, parked curbside in front of Ellspies Pharmacy in Yaptahatchee Springs. We drove over to Seeney's place. The rental car in the driveway had Satan written all over it. I mean seriously. Eustice took a marking pen and wrote S A A T A N in big yellow letters on the hood, the doors, and back of the car. Fucking idiot misspelled it too. There was a woman asleep in the backseat. Shit, was she dead? I opened the door and the stench hit me like a burst of diarrhea after a dozen tacos, and Mexican bottled water. The gal looked like the whore from the "Live Gal on Pony Show." Shit. Whoever's car it was, I think I knew who, had spent days on the road with a hooker. Did I mention she had all sorts of stripper outfits, velour, silk, platform shoes, all colors too? Yes she did.

I began at the beginning. I believed there was such a thing once, but I know better now. At least for me. Redemption? What is it? Some twist, turn, careen around a corner, that'll give your life a redo? Nah, it is what it is. How much quality do you get? A few dabs through decades, maybe more maybe less. If life's being partitioned might as well measure it, right? Happiness? That's a joke. Ha Ha. Funny, not really. Irony is what you get. Transient moments of pleasure, whittled into wretched moments, spiraling into some despair. Only to bounce back, maybe. Sometimes laughing, sometimes crying, all times weary of what's to come. A human life=birth, breeding, training, adaptation, and suppression of primal urgencies. Then stratification and conformity. Finally a automaton, classified, characterized, and pigeonholed for life. A personhood adapted to acceptable parameters of particular culture, or anthropological group. Maybe the constructs of light and dark, night and day, good and evil, are in some grand scheme of things some machination of our own minds to accommodate the positive and negative charges of our building blocks. Our minds simply macroscopic mirrors of the very particles which they're built from: Protons, neutrons, electrons, balancing each other off for a predetermined expanse of time. To serve no other function but to exist within a larger magnetic field. Positive and negative. Forever romanticized, politicized, and made metaphoric.

I considered these things rubbing my wrists, still sore from the handcuffs.

ME AND MR. MEPHISTOPHELES

The sheriff released me from custody once the paperwork was straightened out, and deputies came to search Eustice's rig. Eddy had gotten an attorney, hired a helicopter and sped things up. There was after all an emergency. A crisis he called it.

Luanne was in Seeney's rig, and found remnants of his "visitor" from Hell. Nacho Cheese Doritos, booze bottles, beers cans, vials, and syringes. In what could have been a dorm room at Trailer Park U.

She joined me at land's end and took my hand. I didn't feel much then, nor would I for a long time. What dawned upon me came quickly like a flash-freeze crystallization. A locomotive of thought churned through the rails of my mind. Tracks lain long before I had the steam to ride them. I knew then what I'll know forever, however long that is: Once the universe falls to pieces the reassembly within our mind weighs each part equally. Good, evil, love, hate, occupy the same weight, same strength, until you know what part of the puzzle they belong. And then it hit me like a hard fist at the end of a strong unforgiving arm connecting with my dropping jaw. The North Star began to glitter like the sun. I had to squint, then shut my eyes. It started getting warm, warmer, holy shit. It was like a magnifying glass was aimed right at me. I could smell my own flesh burning. Shit . . . "Luanne!"

* * *

59

Oh my goodness. Oh my, my, my. I do not believe what I am now. I can't, I can't, no. I was standin' there in the middle of nowhere—wherever that was—and I had on clothes that weren't clothes at all! I had on a red suit, a body suit with a hood stuck to my scalp. I felt my head, there was horns on it! Oh Jesus help me help me. I knew it deep down. I know what I'd become. I put my hand where my tush was and felt a collsarn tail comin' out. I knew that I had on a devil suit. Comin' from where I was just at to where I am now, I reckon that whatever super duper powers there was done did somethin' to me that turned me into something I ain't shoulda been. But Heaven ain't gonna help me for sure. I had become the new Satan.

What else was there? Thoughts were put into my thinker brain, and that Coltrane sound resonated like violin strings on a ukulele, at the cemetery, with a full moon.

Shee-yatt. Satan—the original one—done did do a shitty job, and the space critters fired his ass. They knew that I been to Hades, they knew what I knew, and that meant they knew how it all operated.

"That's right, sport." The voice said.

And out of nowhere the bartender from Hell's first stop appeared. That same collsarn rascal who'd come by my place on earth.

"Where the Hell am I?"

"Home, boss."

6 6 6

60

So there I was in Hades major. The bar in Hell. That's the first place you land if you miss the bright white light and see that blurry red fog, and go into a twirl toward Hades. Plop, you land in check. The Hades Bar. I looked around. Smoky, dingy gals, in slacks. Ain't got no artificial breastesses on account they get taken out. No booze, or is there? Elvis, Marilyn Monroe, Kennedy Folk, stadiums of poor credit folks, Alfred Nobel, Einstein, Johnny Cochran, and on and on. And now me! It's feelin' worser and worser knowin' that I am now in charge of all this damnation. Will I have to do bad things to people? Tempt `em, check up on `em while their sleepin', haunt the earth?

"Seeney, don't get ahead of yourself. You have minions to do that for you." Hell's bartender said.

He's the guy with mirrored contact lenses. Tall, lanky crumb bum.

Ain't but even a real body, a figment of my own ideation, or somethin' like that.

"Or something indeed like that, Seeney, er, Master. I think that suits you better, sir. Yes I can indeed read your thoughts."

"Can I make a call?"

"Just have a seat, and I'll arrange a meeting of the board of directors. They'll most certainly want to discuss Hell's new CEO."

"No. This can't be happenin', I ain't evil. I'm a redeemed man. I live a clean life."

"Not anymore boss."

"Stop callin' me that. And get me a drink. A real drink."

"We have work to do sir. There are souls waiting. Remember all of earth's events are measured here. You know all, see all, and have a file on every soul on earth."

"No. No I ain't runnin' credit scores on the new arrivals. Get this suit offa me!" I started tuggin' and pullin' and the material didn't give but for nothin'.

"Eustice, or should I say you're Satanic Majesty, there is no way out of that suit. It has been ordained."

"No, no, no, that's your regular bosses job. He's just indisposed."

"Now, now, Lord and Ruler of he Underworld is an honor."

"I just wanna go home. Back to my trailer and my airboat, and my big screen TV."

"No can do sport, I mean boss. No can do."

666

61

MEANWHILE BACK ON EARTH

He couldn't see and his flesh was smoldering, when Trip Wiley stumbled into the sliding glass door, smashing his nose. Luanne ran toward him, slid it open, and took him in her arms.

"Luanne, something's happened to Eustice."

"Trip, sit down. Let me get you a cold rag."

"No. Not now. I'll be fine. Take me to the refrigerator."

Trip stood in front of the open refrigerator for nearly ten minutes before he spoke.

"Get a flashlight," he said to Luanne.

"Where am I going to find a flashlight, Trip?"

"Just find one." He turned to face her.

"Oh my Lord, look at your face." She stepped back until her butt was pressed against the counter in Seeney's galley.

"What about my face?" Trip put his hands on his cheeks. "Shit, it stings."

"You got a sunburn, a bad one too," she said. "Go look at yourself in the mirror. "And there's like writing or something on your forehead, in the skin."

"Luanne, what the fuck are you talking about?"

"Just go look. Go on look and see for yourself." she said.

Wiley was staring at his face in the bathroom mirror. His ordinarily tanned skin was beet red. Within the blush were tiny lines that had no coloring at all. A hypo-pigmentation of tissues on his forehead lines were configured in such a manner to appear as words. He leaned over the sink and studied the lines on his face, all of them. Someone, something, somehow engraved his facial creases with a chicken-scratch of words. Trip Wiley recognized the writing. "Luanne," he called out.

"What is it?" She stood at the threshold looking at Wiley.

"What does my face say?"

"Trip, I don't understand."

"Luanne, I felt a scorching beam of something out there."

"When you were out by the lake?" She asked.

"Swamp. When I was staring out over the water, a star began pulsing and I felt a burning . . . "

"Sunburn at night? Trip, I think you're losing it," she stepped closer and stared at his face. "There ARE words in your skin."

"What do they say Luanne?"

"I can't tell, it's all squiggly," she narrowed her eyes and came closer.

"I was looking at the North Star, and it began pulsing, getting hotter, and I felt it burn like the sun." Wiley saw her suck in her lip and bite down as he leaned toward her. "Can you make it out?"

"Stars ARE suns, Trip. You know that. But a sunburn at night?"

"Just read what it says, my neck's getting stiff leaning like this. What does it say honey?"

"It's just a few words and they're fading. Help me I am the new boss of Hell, your friend Eustice."

62

"I need a plastic surgeon and an exorcist. Shit, right now. I'm going to have a beer." Wiley said.

"You know Trip, I've been nothing but a two dimensional person throughout this whole thing. Now you want me INVOLVED?"

"Luanne, this is bigger than me, you, or anything else. Can you get me that beer?"

"My aunt dabbles," Luanne said, as she took a Rolling Rock from Seeney's refrigerator, twisted off the cap, and handed it to Wiley. He was reclining on Eustice's favorite lounge chair with a cloth over his face.

"Dabbles?" Trip sat upright, letting the rag fall. "Your aunt in L.A. with the antique shop?"

"She and her boyfriend own one, yeah. She dabbles in tarot card reading, seances, and occult things. You know, a scam."

"That's right she lives with that asshole, Zill Crapmonger. The dope peddling Osteopath to the porn industry. You told me about that."

"Like everything else you didn't pay attention."

"I'm paying attention now." Trip was standing up looking around the room. "Can you call her?" Trip looked at his watch, drummed his fingers on his thigh, and said, "I've been tattooed, look at this shit on my face. Seeney's in trouble and it's three hours earlier in L.A."

"What do you think Aunt Donna and that pervert can do?"

"Send me to Hell." Wiley said,

"What? You sound like a crazy man Trip." She folded her arms across her chest and shook her head. "This is really no quick hop to visit a friend."

"I told you this is not as simple as I thought it would be." Trip said.

At that moment there was knock at the door.

* * *

63

Trip Wiley opened the door and saw a tall man of African descent, and woman who looked like a cross between Lauren Bacall in Key Largo, and Faye Dunaway in the movie Chinatown. She was gorgeous, and the black man could have been a dead ringer for Samuel L. Jackson's character in the movie Shaft. Did they send these people over from some sort of cosmic central casting?

The woman was just glamorous enough, with her long wavy hair, and the man next to her in the trailer parks cheesy yellow light looked as out of place as the white Rolls Royce behind them. They were crowned by Seeney's porch lamp, like glowing regal scarecrows dressed for a banquet. The man's long leather jacket, sunglasses, and beret, had a menacing look, neutralized by her elegance. They were a handsome couple, and Trip knew who they were. "Ellen, Spooky, I was just thinking about you two."

"Here we are." The woman said, in a voice that Trip would recall sounded like sandpaper being dragged over satin sheets. "Are you going to invite us in Trip?"

"Of course," Wiley said, and escorted them into Eustice's den. "This is Luanne," he introduced her to them. "Harold 'Spooky' Pollack, and Ellen K. Hall, meet Luanne. Luanne meet Eustice Seeney's angels."

The explanation was brief: Eustice died, went to Hell a dozen years ago, and met Ellen K. Hall, a frequent visitor to Hades, functioning at the behest of The Powers to locate any unjustly damned. And Spooky, an on again, off again private agent of The Powers, to oversee those on their way to Heaven aren't sidetracked. Sounded simple and straightforward, right? Trip didn't particularly care if Luanne bought it or not, he needed these people here, now, and one more to get done what he had to do.

Luanne looked at the guests: "It's nice to meet you," she said.

"Offer them something to drink, Luanne." Trip said.

What the Hell else is this guy going to want from me? She essentially had enough bullshit. More than enough. All this cosmic Heaven and Hell shit? Please. Should have stayed in Vegas.

"You'd never go far in your acting career, darling." Ellen K. Hall said.

"How do you know?" Luanne, heading for the kitchen stopped, turned, and came face to face with Ellen K. Hall. "What are you a mind reader?"

"Yes, I am. Please continue preparing drinks darling."

Luanne looked at Ellen the way a pole dancer looks at Monopoly money in her garter belt. Bitch. Luanne thought she was way overdressed. An evening gown, a fur stole, and an unlit cigarette in a silver holder dangling from full red lips. Please.

"I could use a light, darling."

Trip broke the tension between the women with a snap of his fingers adding, "Eustice is the new Satan."

"I know, mon." The man named Spooky said.

"Do you have a plan?" Trip asked.

"We took the liberty of arranging a little journey for you Dr. Wiley."

"Journey?"

"Yes. We know that you were going to ask Luanne's aunt and her boyfriend—the medium and the Osteopath—for help, and decided it best we all work together."

"You eavesdropped?" Luanne said.

"Darling, please, just fix us some drinks. We have work to do."

"Time is not our friend here." Spooky looked at his wristwatch. "Soon Eustice will become every bit the Devil his predecessor was."

"You must be kidding." Luanne began tapping her foot. "I think you're all insane. Just plain crazy."

"They should be enroute now." Spooky said. "I believe your Aunt Donna has a deck of tarot cards in her possession."

"How could you know that?" Luanne's eyes bulged. "Nobody knows about that."

"It's a very old deck," the black man said, in a soft knowing tone.

"Even that jerk Zill Crapmonger doesn't know," Luanne rubbed her ankle.

"That scar isn't really a scar darling, is it? You never had the image removed did you?" Ellen said. "It's a crucial card for the deck."

"My aunt's deck of tarot cards?"

Spooky said: "Visconti-Sforza is the name of the tarot deck. It is from the 15th-century, and one of the oldest known to exist. It had a significant impact on the visual composition, card numbering, and interpretation of modern decks, but lacked some cards. Years and years ago we removed one, and we have it. It was our trump card."

"Darling, remember that nice man who offered to removed the tattoo on your ankle?"

"Yes. Well, not exactly. Zill started to, but I wouldn't let him finish. He was drunk, and I decided to live with it. He said I'd never be a porn star with a tarot card tattooed on my leg. I didn't want any of that filth. It's still there."

"No." Luanne said. "Zill?"

"Yes, mon. All is as it should be. She has the missing card right there on her leg."

"I'm confused." Luanne said.

"You should be." Ellen said. "It was the missing card, the Devil Card."

"Oh my . . ." Luanne held her hand over her mouth.

"Trip, once the deck is arranged Luanne's leg will complete it, and we can proceed. We must get them all together for this to happen."

"I'm lost Ellen," Trip said.

"Not too worry sweetheart," she winked at Wiley. "We have it all worked out. We're expediting the journey Zill and Donna will be making. And Luanne, you'll see what happened to the tattoo on your ankle. It's in the deck of cards your aunt is bringing."

"What if she forgets, what if she lost them?"

"Luanne, there are things you leave to chance, and things you don't."

"That's right, mon."

Trip had a look of bewilderment, but finally said: "Now what?"

"We're all going to be meeting up in Miami, to an old clinic darlings." Ellen said.

"Eddy's not practicing. He's a burned out plastic surgeon who still owns a clinic that's better equipped than the most state of the art hospitals. Zill Crapmonger may be a lousy doctor, but he was an anesthesiologist." Trip said.

"For what we have in mind mon, we're going to need at least three physicians. None of them with anything to lose."

"I guess that's me, Eddy, and Zill Crapmonger D.O. drug dealer to the stars."

64

EUSTICE IN HELL

So here I am in Hell, again. Only this time not as a visitor. Shee-yatt! Me, Eustice Seeney, myself, not as a visitor but as the new whoop-tee-do boss of the whole collsarn stinkin' place. I did not ask for this billet. But as a soldier of the Lord I follow orders, and maybe this is where I ought be. Maybe. Or it could be somethin' else, aliens, space critters, Satan gettin fired. They're dummies when it comes to earthly stuff, our Heaven, our Hell. How else could they overlook all those Hindus, Moslems, and Buddhists? Hellfire there's only so many religions folks outside this solar system can give a hoot about, right?

Eh, bull-pucky. Here I am one more time in the pits of the afterlife, not as a guest or hostage. Some alien on some far off planet figured out yours truly had been here before. Writ books about it too. Collsarn aliens must've been the only ones who'd read `em, and they decided to give me the gig: To out-devil the old Devil.

Maybe I ought not have took him out on the swamp. So much for woulda, coulda, shouda's. Listen to me, cryin' the blues.

6 6 6

65

AS I WALK THROUGH THE VALLEY OF THE SHADOW OF THE SAN FERNANDO MOUNTAINS

"Donna, that niece of yours is in some real trouble isn't she?" Zill Crapmonger said. "I don't need a trip to Florida, but this is some jet." They were on a Gulfstream V out of Santa Monica on a direct flight to Miami International.

"I gotta tell you cupcake, whatever that asshole boyfriend of hers is up to, he's got some bank. Private jet, chauffeur at the door five minutes after a call, badabing, yup yup."

"I barely had time to pack. I didn't even bring a swimsuit," Donna said.

"Swimsuit. Shit with the kind of money I'm gonna make, I can buy you a dozen swimsuits, even get that boob job to boot."

"Money you're going to make, Zill?" Donna asked.

"Cupcake, who's the anesthesiology man here?" Zill Crapmonger thumped his chest, and ran a thumb and index finger along the collar of his sport coat. "My freaking money honey, Yup yup."

They were wheels in the air within twenty minutes of the phone call, and Zill into his second Johnnie Walker Blue.

"You do have that bullshit deck of cards, don't you Donna?"

"That IS what the driver asked to see before I could even get in the car." Donna replied.

* * *

66

EUSTICE IS GROOVIN' IN HELL

SatanII. Shee-yatt. I really didn't ask for this. In case anyone's reading this: I do not want this stinker of a job. Nonetheless, I reckon I deserved it pokin' around as I have, right?

So there I was, sittin' on a barstool in Hell's welcome center, a fancy schmancy bar. That's so new arrivals get a cozy sense of the place before the real crappiness kicks in. The last devil runnin' the show set it up so souls maintained an image of themselves, and how other people looked too. There's a mirror across the Lucite counter that's got coins from all over the world embedded in it. Personally I think they're phony, but they do class it up a little. There's pictures on the walls by famous artists: Andy Warhol, Monet, Manet, lots of nekid gals, and porno pictures too. It's all just a big put-on. Once you set down at the bar you can see for yourself that you really ain't got no corporeal body, on account the mirror don't reflect your image back.

That was a real humdinger the first time I saw it. But I CAN see myself, and I don't like what I see. I'll probably freak a few folks out a might, but that IS my job for now. Sort of an official greeter till the minions or whoever's gonna get me adjusted here, show me how to get all devilish. Dead folks are comin' in all the time, after not seein' the bright white light. That's a real frightener! Surprise. There ain't no unicorns, smiley faces, or happy grandparents with open arms. No. This is Hades, and the only horned critter here is me, Eustice Seeney.

"Set me up barkeep," I said to the creep who now worked for me. "I don't want no hooky fanucky, non-alkyhol beer neither. Fetch me the good stuff, Pappy Van Winkle. Chop chop, I ain't got all day." I looked at my hand, and Eww it was a craggily lookin' thing. Long crummy, fungus lookin' nails, and a big signet ring with a red gemstone in it the size of a goat's eye. What have I become? That's Hell for you, always a surprise. The drink arrived, and the bartender bowed as if I was royalty. I reckon I was now.

"Sir," the barkeep said. "The board awaits."

"I'm busy."

"Hell's board of directors and the shareholders are waiting. You have a lot of souls to tend to."

"Blah blah blah. I'm fixin' to finish my drink and chat with some new arrivals." I lied. I had to bail on this gig, tweren't me.

Besides the horns on my head were very uncomfortable, and sitting on a tail? I can only imagine makin' number two.

I looked across the bar. Fancy lookin' place, that's for sure. Must be the most expensive bar a person ever been to, the last one too. I had it all and I gotta say, "this devil outfit was fittin' finer and finer." I was feelin' right good too. Maybe it was the Pappy Van W . . .

I heard a ruckus and turned to look: A big ole hole appeared, and there was a row of people lined up. They was pushin' and shovin' like the lower teeth of a day drinker, all rotten, grimy, and ready to fall out from the shakes. They looked like they stunk somethin' fierce too. Poop and vomit stink. Bleah. Then again this wasn't some disco. They were passin' through what looked like a metal detector, but I knew better. It was a computer screener: It plucked out their memories, mixed and matched 'em with Hell's own, ran a quick credit score, and dispatched the newbies to whatever compartment they belonged for the first part of their eternal damnation.

Hoowee was they in for a ride. I don't right know why, but I was gettin' a warm sensation from my innards. I took another look at myself in the mirror, and those horns was lookin' pretty cool. Pretty collsarn cool. Ha.

6 6 6

67

KEY TO MIAMI

EM. "Eddy" Krazz, MD, or just plain Eddy to his friends, spent his days looking out for numero uno, himself. Too many favors over an abbreviated career, and an eighteen month stretch at Club Fed left him less inclined to go very far out of his way. Other than return a phone call, sit in on a card game, or report in to his parole officer. But that was years ago, and Edward M. Krazz hadn't set foot on the mainland in nearly a decade. As requested, he sent along one of his "assistants," who Trip would suspect was one among many of Eddy's collection: Costa Rican, Brazilian, or Eastern European. Maybe it was the fishnet stockings on long slender legs that stopped mid thigh, a half foot short of her miniskirt. Transparent high heel shoes, and plunging—make that revealing to the point some would call indecent exposure—neckline. This wasn't South Beach where anything goes in terms of attire. After all, she could have been a model, but Trip knew Eddy too well.

Models cost more than hookers, and Eddy despite his millions held on to every dollar like he'd die without it. Of course Trip had sufficient dirt on some of Eddy's "less than wholesome facial transformations," to aide and abet some of Miami's preeminent dope dealers gone legit. That information was reserved in lieu of: fucking over the med school crony. A favor bank for that what-if situation, which this indeed was.

Trip asked the delivery girl who dropped off the keys and alarm codes at Seeney's digs, how long it took her to find the place. Disdain shone past the heavy makeup. She cocked her hip, and looked over a bare shoulder at the Ferrari still idling behind the other vehicles, and said: "Long enough." She notched her chin toward the Rolls, her dark hair bounced across her face. "Silver Wraith, that's like one-of-a kind. Some party you've got going on here." She smiled and struck a suggestive show-your-stuff pose, that required some serious practice. The contortion hiked her skirt expertly, so Wiley could see she had no panties on.

At that moment Luanne appeared, cleared her throat and said, "I like your outfit," with the sincere insincerity reserved for women fighting over the price of a diet soda. "This is a private party," Luanne added.

The dark haired woman bit down on her lower lip, and held up a key and a slip of paper. "I was supposed to bring this to Dr. Wiley."

"That would be me," Trip said holding out his hand, palm up.

She dropped the key, and let the paper drift down. "Where is this place, Hell?"

Luanne snatched it before it hit the ground. "Something like that," she said watching her leave.

They listened as the car's engine revved, backed out, and sped off. Its sound became inaudible after a few moments. "Lets go open up the office and wait for Zill and your aunt."

"If they show," Luanne said.

"They'll show." Trip said confidently.

* * *

68

"Some joint you got here. Gotta run into some serious coinage, eh?" Zill Crapmonger said. He was standing in the waiting room: Knockoff Hugo Boss blazer, sleeves pushed up to his elbows, fake gold Rolex on his wrist, matching pinky ring on his right hand. He blew into it and pointed across the room. "Friggin' cold in here, ain't it?" He notched his chin toward a wall across the room. "Trip, are those real?" He walked across the marble floor, elaborate columns, cornices, plush furniture, and leaned toward an alcove with three oil paintings, pulling off a pair of 2.5 diopter reading glasses and stared. "They fugazi?"

"Zill, Eddy's a collector. Of course they're real. Are you for real?"

"Wiley, don't give me any crap. Dicks like you always givin' me crap. Yup yup."

"Calm down honey, we're in Miami. We're guests, they flew us here on a private jet. My gosh you can be such an ingrate." Donna put her hand on his arm just above the elbow, and drew him closer. "I hope you didn't get too bombed on the plane."

"Don't worry about me cupcake. We're only here because of that bullshit deck of tarot cards. Prized friggin' possession. Like the kid you never had, eh? Magical cards blah blah. Family heirloom my ass."

She pulled away. "Zill, you're drunk. How are you going to do any procedures?"

"Shut the Hell up. A little anesthesia, ten grand—"

"Nobody discussed a fee." Trip Wiley stood up and looked at Crapmonger. "You are buzzed, aren't you?"

"You gonna tell me how to practice Wiley? You can put yourself under—what the fuck ya need me for, know-it-all M fucking D."

Spooky Pollack was seated on one of the sofas across an elaborate coffee table-magazine stand, in the cosmetic surgery center. Shaking his head he put his feet up, crossing one ankle over the other. "You are only here as a guest, Dr. Crapmonger," he said. "That's right, darling." Ellen K. Hall sat next to Spooky and looked across the magazines at Donna, Trip, and Crapmonger. "Did you know Hugo Boss designed the Nazi uniforms?"

"What the Hell is that supposed to mean?" Zill inspected his sleeve, pulled it down, buttoned his jacket, and shrugged, "I don't give a shit lady. Who the fuck are you, Eva Braun? You look like you've had more plastic surgery than all the old whores in . . . "

She flung her hand out like she was casting a spell. To Wiley it looked like something must have hit him in the gut, because Zill crumpled over like he'd been punched.

"Shit." Donna said. "Why'd you do that? He's old"

Donna stepped over to Crapmonger, put her arm around him, and led him to one of Eddy's waiting room chairs."

"I'm not old dammit! Get me one of my pills! Yup a pill would be good, and somethin' to wash it down with cupcake."

"Crapmonger's worthless," Wiley said, watching Donna take a vial out of his jacket pocket."And stoned. Some gas passer."

"He's on medication you know. Have some patience." Donna unscrewed the childproof top. "Time released—"

"OxyContin? Friggin' pain meds, coated, tamper-proof pills, plus booze? Moron probably prescribed it himself," Wiley said. "He'll be sufficiently useless for a while. Shit."

"Relax Trip, just be patient." Spooky reached across to help Crapmonger get comfortable.

"Just relax. Now Donna, please hand me the deck." She would later recall staring at his long dark fingers, he wasn't asking at all. In fact she felt a chill. Just as the elegant woman tossed her head back, long waves falling behind her. Slowly she brought herself face to face with the antique dealer from the San Fernando Valley, and let out a mirthless laugh. The lights flickered and the doors to the exam rooms shut at once in a collective "whomp." Donna would swear they did it, just then.

"The cards darling. We don't have all night." Ellen said.

"We best get moving to one of the Operating Rooms," Eddy said, looking at his watch. "Down this corridor, come on follow me, we need to get ready for this."

"Thash a fack. Yup yup." Zill stumbled forward.

"Lay him down out in the lobby," Donna suggested.

"I'm not freaking tired and you need me. You better believe it, you need my skill." Zill muttered.

"Calm down, Zill," Donna said. "Just sit down."

"No we need him." Spooky said

Eddy looked at the black man, nodded and said, "Spooky's right, it's the middle of the night. A passed out man in the Full Cleveland, bad rug, and smelling like patchouli would be bad for business."

Eddy stared at Crapmonger. "What the fuck are those things around your neck, douchebag?"

"Here we go," Eddy said. "Everyone all set, I know I am."

"You ain't got shit," Zill said softly.

Eddy considered decking him on principal alone.

* * *

69

MEANWHILE BACK IN HELL

Board of Hell's Trustees. Ha. I was too busy right now. Them folks flowin' on in was too much of a hoot to stop watchin'. All of them souls was gonna be mine, and it felt right good havin' all that power.

I don't reckon I gotta to rush on over to no dumbo meeting. I AM the boss here. I'm groovin' on this gig. Look at those folks comin' in. Bunch of crumb bums if you ask me, and nobody's askin'. I am the chief of all this. And the booze? Top notch.

"Barkeep, git your lazy butt movin' and fetch me another."

"Sir, the board cannot wait for all eternity—"

"Bull-pucky barboy, they can wait as long's I say they can. I am the new and improved leader of the Underworld."

I tell you that bein' the Devil is one humdinger of a job. "Git me a computer screen, not nary no dumbass smartphone. The special one. The one my predecessor had whooped up."

"But sir . . ." the barkeep slapped his palms on his thighs like some Hell bird tryin' to flap its Hell wings, but twasn't goin' noplace, on account Hell's Hell. That skinny little weezer had me to reckon with, and ain't no way had a choice. "Boy," I said real slow, twirlin' my glass on the counter. "I want you to git that sorry ass of yours back behind the bar, and fetch me some more Pappy."

He did. Ain't had no choice, me bein' who I'd become. Damn this suit was feelin' good. Reminded me of when Doc Wiley took me out shoppin' for some duds, way back when I had to go to court. Yes siree, that was a long ways back. I'd been the subject of "medical errors," and them folks on the jury couldn't give me more money. I had one fancy go-to-meeting suit some eye-talian homeo whoop'd up right special, and it felt like my own skin. Only this devil suit felt even better. I ain't figured out what the tail's for, and these horns must be like antennas. The tips are a might pointy, and if I twist `em a bit, get a little static in my thinker brain. Ain't got it figured out yet, but I ain't right ready to start hearin' voices in my head yet.

6 6 6

70

TO THE OPERATING ROOM

Eddy guided Trip, Luanne, Donna, Ellen, Spooky, and Zill "in the bag" Crapmonger, into the operating suite.
"Listen folks, I'd like you all to put on some scrubs. You'll find them in the locker room. Then there are a few other things we need to go over before we go into the OR for this procedure. Trip will help, right Tripper?"

"Sure Eddy. Listen folks this is Eddy's operating room, and even though we're not going to be doing any cutting procedures, we need to be prepared for an eventuality."

"What are you saying Trip? I don't understand?" Luanne said.

"Just do as I do. I'm an expert." Zill muttered.

"Thirty years ago," Eddy mumbled.

"Whazzat, hotshot?"

"Nothing. When was the last time you put someone under Zill?" Eddy asked.

"I'll put you under, you little shit."

"Trip, put a leash on that puppy. I don't want him messing up my place." Eddy said.

"Let's just get changed," Trip said. "I think this is Eddy's locker room down this corridor."

"What do need to do Trip?" Donna asked.

"In general: people in the operating room wear surgical clothes to help prevent germs from invading surgical incisions, or in this case inserting some tubes. Skin will be broken, and we don't want to risk an infection. The surgical clothing includes: a protective cap covers the hair, masks over the lower face covering mouths and noses, glasses or goggles over the eyes, Latex gloves on the hands, long gowns, and of course protective covers for your shoes. Eddy's practice has a high volume of surgery, and we don't want to bring in any extraneous organisms."

"You're a friggin' extraneous organism, Wiley. Know it all." Zill took another pill.

"Would you cut it out Zill?" Donna pursed her lips and shook her head. "Right now. We have work to do."

"Darlings," Ellen K. Hall took her flask out and passed it around. The only taker was Zill.

"I'll take some of that, sugar." Zill said.

* * *

It was a "state-of-the-art" operating suite: Spacious, windowless, and temperature controlled. Special air handlers filter the air, and maintain a slightly elevated pressure. Easy to clean tiled walls and floor. Well-lit via an array of overhead surgical lights and viewing screens. Elaborate monitors with displays and sensors. Processing components, display devices, as well as communication links, for displaying or recording the results through a monitoring network.

The operating room was a few degrees cooler than the waiting room Electricity had the usual backup generators in case of a power-out.

"You'll dig this Tripper," Eddy hitched his thumbs in imaginary suspenders. "Check out my operation: The rooms all have the latest wall suction, we do a lot of Liposuction. New state laws dictate how much fat we can suck out. Pretty wild, eh?"

"That's gotta suck, Eddy."

Wiley looked around the OR. "Impressive setup Eddy."

"Thanks Tripper. Only the best for the beautiful people of South Florida, and this is my favorite OR, even though I haven't used it in a few years."

"That little problem, right."

"I thought it was little." Eddy said.

"I guess the state board didn't."

"Eh, I prefer to leave the grunt work to my staff anyways. I've gotten used to sleeping in, dig?"

"I hear you Eddy. Let's familiarize the group with things before we . . ."

"Trip, I'm not really sure what you're planning, but you know about the zone I'm in, and—"

"Nobody's gonna get hurt Eddy. Maybe me, but it'll only be for few minutes. Remember that movie where those medical students made each other dead?"

"Flatliners? "Young Julia Roberts, Kevin Bacon, shit. You're gonna pull a Bacon aren't you?"

"Relax Eddy. See those two?" Wiley pointed at Ellen and Spooky with his chin. "They've got juice."

"What kind of juice?" Eddy asked.

"The kind that'll make sure you were never here, if the shit hits the fan."

"Tripper, I don't know about . . . "

"Ten million US dollars. Go on check your account on Grand Cayman," Spooky said.

"How do you know about that?" Eddy said, pulling out his smartphone.

"I'll show these folks around and get things ready Eddy, while you check your bank account." Trip said. "I'm sure you'll be cool with that."

Trip gave Ellen, Spooky, Luanne, and Donna a tour. Zill sat on a gurney with Ellen's flask. "I know this shit like the back of my hand. Go on." Zill slurred.

The operating room had the usual: oxygen and other anesthetic gases, operating table, and anesthesia cart. Mayo stands to set up instruments, storage space for common surgical supplies, and containers for disposables. Outside the operating room are dedicated scrub sinks, and a lounge used by surgeons, surgeon's assistants, anesthetists, and nurses to gather prior to surgery.

Trip explained a few things every now and then, as he walked through Edward's elaborate facility. "An operating room will have a map.

Enabling the terminal cleaner to realign the operating
table and equipment, to the desired layout after cleaning.
Edward has several operating rooms that are part of the
operating suite of the clinic. They form a distinct section
within the facility, which is closely regulated by the state.
There ARE surprise investigations from time to time."

"I suppose that's one of the things that tripped up your
good buddy, isn't it Trip?" Luanne said.

"Really Luanne. This isn't the time or place."

"Moving along: besides the operating rooms, there are
rooms for personnel to change, wash, and rest.
Preparation and recovery rooms, storage, cleaning
facilities, offices, dedicated corridors, and other
supportive units. The operating suite is intricately
climate and air-controlled, and separated from other
departments, to prevent any organisms from spreading."

Eddy's face lit up from the phone's screen. Holy shit who
are these people? He said to himself, as he passed
Crapmonger to join the sightseers. "Hey wait up," Eddy
shouted. "I think everything will be just fine. And you,"
he said to Crapmonger, "Get up and make yourself
useful."

Zill managed to pull himself together to examine the
Anesthesia machine. "Ish all in order." He held up his
hands. "Look at how new thish shit is," he said, staring at
the mechanical respiratory support.

"Look at that ventilator and Johnny on the spot O2 support. Shiet, I can't wait to get ready to get going."

Eddy looked at Crapmonger, and shook his head. "Trip, I can't believe this jerk. He's going to fuck up my OR."

Zill kept rambling: "Thish is for administering anesthetic gases, which I can use for some light sedation." He raised his hand and said, "Or woo, deep and total anesthesia." Crapmonger stumbled into the anesthesia cart. "Yes siree Edward, you got all the latest." Zill examined the containers, all were up to date. "Look at the extra IV push meds for anesthesia, sedation and reversal. Extra equipment that I'll be giving. Everything I need, and even shit I might not need. It ish very important for the anesthesia tools to be well organized and maintained, so that patients receive proper anesthesia care. You know that?" Zill said, just as the time released medicine kicked in.

"Let's put Wiley on the table. You ready for this Tripper?" Eddy said.

* * *

71

The operating table in the center of the room was raised and tilted slightly, with Trip's legs higher than his head. The operating room lights over the table provided bright light, without shadows. Ellen patted her locks and said, "I feel like I'm on the set."

"You are Ellen." Spooky said unceremoniously.

Zill looked at the anesthesia machine at the head of the operating table. "Just like the old days. This machine's got tubes that connect to the patient, Wiley over there, to assist his breathing during the procedure. What's the procedure anyways?"

"Shut up Crapmonger. Just step away from the monitors. I don't want you fucking with the controls that deal with the mixture of gases in the breathing circuit. I can do that. You're too fucked up."

"I'm a Board Shertified Anesthesiologist, dammit!" Zill grabbed the paddles off the defibrillator. "I know my shit dammit." He stared at the cart next to the Anesthesia machine, inspecting the medications and equipment. "I know what I'm doing."

"Sit down, Zill." Ellen said.

"Shirt off buddy." Eddy said to Wiley. He began applying adhesive "leads" to his chest, attached to an electronic monitor to record heart rate. "Finger." he said. Wiley watched as he placed a clip atop his digit, to the pulse oximeter machine. Eddy explained to the crew: "This measures the amount of oxygen contained in the blood. There's an automated blood pressure machine, that inflates the blood pressure cuff on Trip's arm." Eddy pushed away the electrocautery machine. It uses high frequency electrical signals to cauterize, or seal off blood vessels. "We won't be needing this." Eddy moved with a "ten million dead president's" spring to his steps.

"I gotta admit Eddy. I'm a little freaked out." Trip said.

"Me too, pal. Me too." Eddy whispered. "Lay back, okay. I'll get some diazepam."

* * *

72

BACK IN HELL

"Oh there's my drink Barboy, you done good. Now go tell the barmaids to come over here and line up. I wanna check `em out." I got to wonderin' if my johnson, my new Satanafied johnson that is, was as devilish as the rest of me. I felt somethin' twitchin', as I watched folks comin' in from their evil way'd life. Hoowee there was some real winners in that crowd. They sure's didn't expect to be here, no siree. Oh they still had bodies, you could see. On account in the afterlife: that energy we had, remains projected. This was explained to me by a real smart fella, so they remain for further judgments. If they was burnt up in a fire, exploded, or mutilated, the cosmos patches together some rough approximation. But their "aura" remains as crummy as it was, that'd got `em damned. Look at these folks. Hoowee, a nonstop line of `em on their way to get allocated. I can see how the old Satan got sick of this part of the gig, and had his minions do it. They were one sorry battalion of bozos, who'd broken more Commandments than considered passable. I'd have to reckon "D" student, dead folks. Lugubrious walkin' folks, lookin' like scaredy cats. May've been hotshot, wheeler dealers, up on earth. Gangsta, thug, punk kids, about to lose those gold chains, and droopy pants. Painted ladies about to get uglified. Do I really have to do that? Shee-yatt. I don't know how I knew the rules of this place, but knew them nonetheless. I was waitin' for the computer. Where the Hell was that punk? I gotta use Hellbook, see who's who down here, and maybe unfriend a bunch of `em.

"Hey barkeep what's the holdup?" I hollered out in my mind's voice. Oh yeah, you get these telepathical powers, on account most folks ain't got no corporeal bodies here. Iffen you did, it was only temporary. That much I knew as a fact. On account, when I was here last time, my own flesh and bones up there was alive on a respirator. If that would've got shut off, I'd have never gotten a bite of earth's finest apples.

"Barkeep, where in . . . are you?"

666

73

IN THE CLINIC

Trip Wiley stared at the ceiling from the operating table calculating what the monthly overhead must be, and every thought or two got hammered with the question: "What the fuck am I doing?" Which really made no difference because he was about to die.

"Darling," Ellen K. Hall had her hand on Trip's forearm, inches away from the IV that Eddy started himself. No staff was going to be in on this deal, not in the middle of the night. "We'll be looking after you. Spooky and I are right here. Nothing can go wrong if you do exactly as we say. Isn't that right Edward?"

"Shit, lady, I own this center. This is where I make my bank. Fifty employees, six doctors, and thousands of procedures. I'm out on a limb here." Eddy said.

"Shut up Eddy. You're not out jackshit. You don't even practice anymore, just collect a check every month.

There's nothing anyone can do to you. For cryin' out loud. You live on a yacht, and you're not even a US citizen anymore." Trip yelled anxiously.

"Fuck you Wiley, I'm as American as the next guy." He nudged a hitchhiker's thumb toward the silent black man, who was now leaning against the operating room's tiled wall. "That guy's here too, shit. What the fuck's with that?"

* * *

"Donna, it is time to place these cards on Dr. Wiley's chest," Spooky said. "We are going to need Luanne to sit on the table with him. Her leg stretched out, exposing the ankle with the tattoo of the missing card."

"Say what?" Crapmonger barged in. "You're all fruitcakes."

"Darling, calm down. Have another drink. We're going to place Trip into a medically induced coma." Ellen said.

"Oh no you're not," Luanne said. Standing between Zill, Eddy, and the table Wiley was on."

"Relax, honey." Trip said. "This has to be done. I'm just going to be asleep for a few minutes."

"What if they can't bring you back? Zill's useless, look at him. He's wasted." Luanne said frantically.

"Fuck that. I'll start the IV. What proshedure are you doing?" Crapmonger stumbled, and fell into the continuous electrocardiogram. Knocking vials of medications for amnesia, analgesia, muscle paralysis, and sedation flying across the tile floor. A Mayo stand with syringes and laryngoscope clattered then shattered.

"You really want me to lay a tarot on his chest?" Donna asked, looking at the elegant lady.

"I'll take care of it," Ellen said. "I know exactly what needs to be done. Now you sweetheart," she said to Luanne, "I need to see that ankle."

"Tashoo?" Zill bent over to grab Luanne's ankle, and fell forward grabbing the paddles and cords of the automatic external defibrillator.

"Help him up," Donna said.

"I don't need no stinking help. I can do thish myshelf," Zill proceeded to climb to his knees, and started turning dials and adjusting levers.

A high pitch shrill permeated the room.

Wiley sat up, the cards fell to the ground. Luanne lost her balance and fell to Trip's side.

ME AND MR. MEPHISTOPHELES

Zill pissed himself.

"Dammit Crapmonger. Go get a fucking mop you slob." Eddy yelled.

"You just hate Osteopaths." Zill, struggling to get up, grabbed the defibrillator, twisting the knob hard clockwise.

"Just you asshole." Eddy said, and kicked Crapmonger in his left flank.

"What the fuck are you doing?" Trip yelled.

At that moment Zill dropped a paddle in the pool of urine and electrocuted himself.

* * *

74

In Hades: Eustice looked up from the bar to see flashing lights above the portal people entered the hereafter from. I was just about fixin't to go over to the board meetin' when I saw it. And if I wasn't already in Hell thought for sure I was gonna get arrested or somethin' worse. But what's worse than already bein' in Hell? I saw them folks all lined up lookin' like critters up to get slaughtered. Shee-yatt, it ain't that bad, it's only eternity here, and there's plenty to keep you busy.

What the Hell was goin' on, I asked myself? He heard an Ahooga horn blast over and over again. Like some collsarn French fire engine or Eastern Europe Police squad out in full force.

666

75

ZILL'S DEAD

Zill Crapmonger sobered up faster than you could say "roadside sobriety test." But nobody was going to ask for him to show his driver's license, or proof of insurance. They weren't going to ask him to blow into a breathalyzer either, because he wasn't breathing. For the first time since he had his first hair plugs under general anesthesia, Zill, had an out of body experience, and something told him that this time he might not be going back. He saw the operating room from above. He saw himself laying there as he floated farther from the people he was with. That schmuck Eddy had a shit-eating grin on his face, and Trip, that son of a bitch, had gotten off the operating table and started compressions on his . . .Shit. On my fucking chest. Luanne had her arms crossed in front of her, and those two freaks, Ellen and Spooky, what the fuck was with them? He couldn't see them, they just disappeared. Where the fuck were they? Then he heard Donna. Lovely Donna with her sweet voice. He could hear her saying something.

He watched her walk up to Wiley, and heard her sigh. Finally saying: "Is that asshole finally dead? I hope there's somewhere to dump him. I'm not paying for any lousy funeral for this jerk." She sounded relieved. He watched Eddy put his arm around her. What the fuck?

The next thing he knew he had left the operatory in Miami, and entered a vast expanse. He knew but he didn't know exactly how he knew—he was going to see the promised land, the bright white light. He knew it as he knew the color red, was the color red. Then it hit him like a bad piece of sushi. He wanted to vomit. All the years of his life, but had none left. He had no body, and there wasn't a bright white light. Out of nowhere he was surrounded by a blurry maroon swirling tunnel, that drew him in. Round, and round, and round he went. Zill couldn't imagine how long he tumbled and spun, but it seemed like forever. Finally he stopped and plopped out of the dark tunnel. Like what he imagined as a turd out of an elephant's butt. He didn't hear himself squish or splatter. He just sat there and wondered briefly just where "there" was. There was a man standing next to him in a Halloween costume.

"Hellfire boy, you look like you had the winning lottery numbers, but played `em on the wrong day." The man in the costume said.

Zill stood up and looked at the man in the Devil suit. Then over at the line of people passing through the metal detector-like portal into the bar room.

He stood up, brushed himself off, and looked behind him. The tunnel he'd just fallen from was still swirling. It seemed, at least to Zill Crapmonger, like some digestive system of a large animal. "Did I come through there?" He hitched a thumb toward the dark gateway. "What the Hell is that, the universe's bunghole? I need a drink."

"No dummy, you must've done somethin' fierce on earth. On account the universe plum made a special gateway just for you. A collsarn tailor-made turnstile. Shee-yatt, you bypassed all them other folks waitin' in line, like a kid that cut in front of everyone else at Disney World. You must've done some right crummy stuff in your life."

"Hang on there Mr. Trick-or-treat, are you tellin' me I'm . . . " Zill Crapmonger paused, pondered, and then recalled the defibrillator paddles, the operating room, and floating over his body.

"Dead. Yes siree buddy, you're done dead. Go on, look at the mirror, you ain't gonna have no reflection. On account you ain't got no corporeal body no more."

Zill craned his neck and looked at the smoky mirror behind the row of bottles at the bar. Relieved at first there were other people there. He turned, twisted, and contorted like he was shadow boxing, finally stopping. "I've got no friggin' reflection!"

"Nope. You just got what's called remnants. That's the stuff left over after you die."

"You can imagine stuff, like the barkeep over there, a real crumb bum. And the barmaids ain't got no false titties."

"Why?" Zill was scatching his head.

"No fake tits allowed in Hades."

"Who the Hell are you?" Zill asked.

"Me? I'm the collsarn Lord and Ruler of the Underworld, you stinker. You broke the collsarn credit checker on your way in, you know that?"

"What?" Zill asked.

"It's the initial screener for newcomers. To see which compartment you get started at. Get used to it, and don't go breakin' nothin' else, you collsarn doody head!"

"Doody head?"

"That hole you came in through's still swirlin'. Collsarn thing ought be shut. Look at that. The tunnel you rode in on from earth to Hell is wide open. Who knows what else can get pooped out." Eustice looked around. "It's crowded in here now. Maybe you left somethin' in there?"

"What the fuck are you talking about. I just fucking died. I don't have dick, you horn headed hillbilly. There's nothing in that fucking hole. Go see for yourself."

"I gotta inspect that," Eustice said, nudging toward the tunnel.

It was dark and seemed to rotate like some living organism. He stood right at its edge.

"I gotta get this thing closed on up. 'Barkeep', Eustice commanded, get this fixed. Some idiot can fall right into it." "Hold this asshole." Seeney gave Crapmonger his glass of Pappy, and said, "Don't go snarfin' my liquor you sumbitch, that's top shelf stuff. Now I gotta figure out how to patch this up."

Zill sniffed the glass, and chugged it down. "Fuck you idiot," he said to Seeney.

Eustice shoved him. Zill shoved back. Eustice whipped his tail around and Zill grabbed it. "How do like that asshole?" Crapmonger said.

"What are you doin' buddy? You're in H E double hockey sticks, HELL, and I'm the new collsarn boss of this place you ninny. Now let go of my tail, dammit!" Eustice was pulling hand over hand on his tail, against Crapmonger's grip. "Let the Hell go or I'll zap a lightning bolt on that scraggly head of bad fake hair!"

At that, Zill let go of the tail, and pushed Seeney into the swirling vortex. Seconds later with a tremendous whomp, the portal shut.

The bartender from Hades bar stood there, looking Crapmonger over.

"That idiot DID fall through—yup yup—good riddance. Wait a second, who the fuck are you?" Crapmonger said to the robotic man dressed like he was out of 1920s central casting .

"Welcome to Hades, I'm in charge of the welcome center, sport."

"Real Gasby shit, huh? Lemme outta this place."

"That is not going to happen, sport."

At that, a presence filled the room. Not man nor beast. Pure unfettered energy came in a tremendous wave. A totality of all overtook and commanded the space. A silence hung in the chamber, and everyone ceased all motion. Even Zill froze. Finally a melodious voice came from everywhere, but nowhere: "Alas, I am finally back where I belong. And you—"

Crapmonger felt eyes look him over. "Who the fuck are you supposed to be?" He asked.

"Who do you think I am? You'll have all eternity to guess who that is. Ha."

6 6 6

76

EUSTICE BACK ON EARTH . . . (MAYBE)

I was spinnin' and spinnin' somethin' fierce, for as long as I could hold on. Then it all stopped, and I felt somethin'. Yuck.

Warm, wet, and squishy, I felt like I'd awoken from pissin' myself on a waterbed filled with hot rum. It was makin' me twitch, and start sweatin' somethin' fierce. I couldn't open my eyes, but I could feel my arms and legs, just couldn't move 'em right. My whole body is in some goopy stuff, like maple syrup or molasses. I raise my arm to my face and it feels all rubbery, my ears are plugged up, and I can't breathe. What the . . .

I forced myself to open my eyes. It's blurry and everything's dark, darker than night's darkest hour. I start movin' my arms and legs against a resistance. Like I got on a rubber suit, and weights on my wrists and ankles. I set into movin', and feel like one them fat people must, when they're tryin' to jog in a plastic runnin' suit.

Shee-yatt! I am underwater. I finally get my eyes open, and see the quilt of the water's surface. Beyond it is a glimmering sphere up in the sky. Am I alive, or am I dead in a new kind of Hades? I don't know how I'm breathin', but my chest hurts. I start flailin' like a frog, or some other water critter, tryin' to get to what's on above me. I don't know how I knew it, or if I knew at all. Maybe it was just instinct, but I needed air. I was only conscious for a few seconds, and didn't have time to think of nothin'. Not where I was, or how I got here, but I knew I'd surely be someplace dark again if I didn't get a move on. I swear that my chest was gonna explode, like a pair of fake titties that'd been overinflated at the gas station. Pumped up is how my body felt. I think my brain was gonna explode. I flipped and flopped my arms and legs, like a spastic tadpole, that ain't got its fins. Or a sperm that only got one tail flagellatin', and this one was crumped up. I don't right know if I was gonna blank back out to the nothingness I was in. I could see I was gettin' closer to the bottom of that blanket up top. The closer I got the fuller my innards was, with foul, stinky, Hellacious funk. Yes, I knew I'd just left a very foul place. As I stroked and swam I rubbed a hand over my head. At that moment I felt relieved. I no longer had them horns on my head.

Somehow, someway, I been sprung from Hades once more. I couldn't let myself just die here. Whatever was beyond the water's surface seemed to be gettin' farther and farther away with each splurge of my arms and legs.

ME AND MR. MEPHISTOPHELES

After a few dozen awkward, disynchronus strokes, my arms and legs got syncopated. At the same time my thorax filled with more and more tension. Would I make it? If so, what was I gonna find.

I had to push harder. Finally my fingers reached a boundary. What if it was ice, and I was trapped beneath it forever? I jabbed my hand up with all that I'd had left in me, and the surface broke. I let out whatever I had in my innards, and my head popped out onto a ripplin' sea of glass, beneath a moon so bright I thought it was the sun. I took in air, earth air, lots and lots of it, like the greatest treasure I'd ever known. I could breathe. And by now could flap my arms and legs. Like I'd been born again as some amphibious being. I watched the waves I'd created reverberate over the water's surface, and lay there on my back lookin' up at the moon. I did it. I was pert near dead, and come back one more time. I was like a pebble that'd been tossed into the water, but instead of bein' tossed in from atop, I got tossed up from below.

I don't right know how long I lay there, but after a spell began to swim. I didn't see no shore or nothin' when I started, but kept movin' nonetheless. I didn't recognize the place at first, but after a while knew I was in one of the big ponds within the Everglades. Some of the patches of mangrove looked familiar. With each pull of my arms, and frog's kick of my legs, things became more and more like I been there before. I saw the outlines of what looked like my airboat not too far away, but knew distances could be discombobulated in that optical delusional way.

I started movin' faster with each glimmer in my mind's eye, that it was my very own airboat. And that there was somethin' I had to do, ticklin' the inside of my skull. I wasn't here just out of luck, it was for a purpose. And I had a meeting with—for lack of anything better—destiny.

Faster and faster I kept thinkin' somethin' urgent was about to happen, and I had to be there. When I felt something stir beneath me. I felt a nibble on my right leg. I thought it was the water on my jeans. I knew they were my old blue jeans, not that dumbass devil suit. And for a second, smiled inwardly. But that didn't last, because that nibble became a squeeze, and then it became a grip. Then I knew I'd been sized up as grub for a bull gator layin' wait, for just some critter that'd swam past its snout, and that was me. I tried kickin' it with my other leg, but it already went into the death twirl, takin' me with it. Round and round they go, killin' a mammal by drownin' and leavin' `em beneath the surface in the roots of some gator nest, to feast on later. I had to fight, and this was gonna be my last.

* * *

77

WHERE THE LAND MEETS THE WATER

It was one of those mornings when the sky's blueness was so blue, it could hold on tight to anyone's imagination of what a perfect sky should be. There were no clouds, and a silence accompanied the stillness. The water's surface smooth and mirror-like. The man at land's end stood there, and took a pack of Marlboro's out of his pocket, put one in his mouth, and lit it. He inhaled and let out the smoke calmly, and watched the smoke rise vertically. He had not been to this place. But if he imagined what a serene place on earth could be, this indeed would fit the bill. He was an average height man with a forgettable face, unremarkable presence, and if there were any other people around he would just blend in with them. As there was nothing extraordinary, remarkable, or striking other than his hat. Which wasn't uncommon in these parts, and the rifle cradled across his chest. It was a marksman's weapon. And upon inspection it was not anything anyone could find in any arsenal in any army, in any nation on the planet.

The man held the cigarette between his thumb and forefinger the way caricatured foreigners do. Silly little things cigarettes, but oddly a unique albeit rotten, use of tobacco plants. But this was not the man's concern. He stood and watched from his station across the waterway, for a period of time that made even the avian critter curious. The morning bird calls would sound more curious than confrontational, in that: "Cheap cheap what the fuck is that human doing sort of way birds would talk if birds could talk. Maybe a passerby, which there was one, Elmo Bazzer. He was doing his usual, snooping. Looking through his binoculars from the adjoining lot, from his mobile home's kitchen window.

Elmo maintained a "hate Seeney" vigil on general purposes. After Eustice accidentally sprayed his yard with insect repellent, which wasn't that at all. Eustice mistakenly used DayGlo, the brand name paint indiscriminately, to ward off "demon bugs," which in fact were part of Elmo's special bait farm. Oh well, revenge was a dish Elmo planned serving on a plate gone cold. And this morning a man with a gun, after all the comings and goings of the last few days, could make for just such a perfect storm. To get his own brand of comeuppance.

What was this stupid hunter waiting for? What the Hell was he doing all dressed up too? Elmo took out his own Mossberg 500 Persuader Shotgun. Yes siree, this 5 + 1-round pump action shotgun, was comfort and control out here.

Elmo was well aware that the universal sound of racking a shell into the chamber this morning, would most certainly scare the shit out of this smoking douchebag friend of Seeney's. Fuckem. He held the synthetic black stock and began planning his route. From tree to tree, creeping up on this sumbitch. Maybe he'd shoot him, and let that asshole Seeney take the heat. Elmo knew the terrain better than the squirrels, opossum, or any critters, and could sneak up just swell. He already had on his camo pants, boots, and khaki muscle shirt. Elmo took to sleeping in his clothes years and years ago, when his wife left him for another postman. Fucker. Should have shot him. Then again he got off clean when that bitch left him with the retirement digs.

He took a swig of Old Grandad, and waited. That guy'd been standing there for a long time. He wasn't goin' nowhere. There was something about this. He did after all, wear a slick looking piece of headgear. Maybe a prize worth taking. Shit, if push came to shove and he had to shoot him dead, Elmo would indeed do it without conscience. That part of him eroded, after years and years of delivering mail to the snotty pricks up in Palm Beach along the ocean, who NEVER left but a thing for him come Christmas. Fuckers. Unfair world, unfair people. Besides what's a little blood on your hands, if you hunt and strip your own food? Nothing. You could probably toss his carcass to the swamp. Gator meat. Ha. Something came over Elmo today that had been building for years. And this seemed, by the third swig of whisky, to be just fine. But now he had to pee. Dammit.

78

The air was warm, but not hot. There was slight humidity, but not much. It was to any passerby, a picture postcard glimpse of all that's beautiful on the planet. The singing bugs of summer, were either resting, or not rubbing their wings. Crickets, Katydid, and Cicadas would wait till day's end for the chorus to begin their buzzy, raspy, whiney calls. If they started up now, what lurked beneath the surface: gators, predators, and any of many eaters of their kind, might just break the water's surface, and snatch `em on up. Snack food. Bugs didn't make much of a meal for the swamp's meat eaters. And despite some of their 120 decibel sounds they "weren't but nothin' to feed the big critters." So the small animals of the swamp, and domesticated ones, dogs, cats, even a small child, could land in the jaws of one of the ancient swamp dwellers. The stillness gave a sense that all was well with life on the edge of the Everglades. The surface of the water at land's end was flat, and reflected the sun's morning light penetrating the dense fluid of what lie beneath the surface. There was a glint in the distance, and some activity. It was motion, violent thrashing about in the water. Elmo saw a real ruckus out on the swamp. Something was going on. He watched as whatever it was sent ripples across the surface, which became waves. The water slapped the shore, drenching the roots with each surge against the shoreline. The roots of the mangrove, leaves, and garbage were drenched. Dead fish fluttered when the waves receded. Something was up. The man in the hat held up his weapon, took aim, and fired.

The silence broke with a blast that would have carried for miles if it wasn't muffled by the swamp's foliage. A natural suppressor. An echo hung in the crystal blue morning, and remained in the air like a phantom with no house to haunt. There was just a slight breeze that blew across the now still water. Leaves rustled, tree trunks groaned, and critters scuttled.

The gator that had him by the leg had been shot, and Eustice lay there listening to the lingering sound of the weapon that had been fired. He swam the breaststroke to shore, dragging his body, careful not to kick overly hard to stir up another gator.

* * *

79

As much as Elmo despised Eustice and all his shenanigans, he hated trespassing assholes more. "Standin' my ground," he said in that not quite belligerent tone, reserved for three billowing sheets to the wind. His mind's jib sail was filled with booze. "You could have at least invited me to one of your fancy whoop-de-do parties Seeney." He grabbed his Persuader and ran out toward Seeney's yard dodging from tree to tree. Jaw fixed and flush with rage, he ran toward the man with the rifle, but felt something wet and moist on him. Damnit. He noticed he'd spilt urine on his unzipped camos. Dammit! He stumbled onward, tripped over the serpentine tentacled roots of an ancient ficus tree, and split open his forehead. He tasted the salty blood flowing down his face, and his vision blurred. Shit, he was losing it. Had to get up and get that son of bitch, but before he could shout: "I'm gonna get you Seeney," he noticed the man who was smoking, staring at him.

His eyes bore through the curtain of blood now filling his view. He couldn't make out his features. The man said one word before he lost consciousness: "Ha."

Elmo was puzzled. Either the blood screwed up his vision, or he was fading fast. He would later recall, the man seemed to have collapsed like an accordion into the ground, leaving nothing but his cowboy hat.

Eustice crawled crab-like over the litter filled embankment, grabbing at the thicket of vegetation. One after another the plants gave way, sending him back into the swamp. Finally, he got his hands wrapped around some thick anaconda shaped roots, and climbed hand over hand onto land. He lain on his back prostrated, staring at the endless sky. Finally he gathered his strength, and brought himself to an erect position, raked his hand through his hair—no horns—and wrung himself like a wet dog. When he'd finally righted himself, Seeney, looked around and saw Elmo laying twenty or so yards away, bloodied, gun by his side. They locked eyes for a moment before Elmo lost consciousness. Doody head neighbor. He shook his head and considered that tweren't no shotgun that killed the gator. Not from this distance, no way. Seeney knew it like he knew his airboat specs. He fanned his arm, exhausted from his swim to shore, looked down at the white cowboy hat, and strange rifle. His leg was bloodied, but he didn't feel much pain. He raised the weapon, examined it, and then the hat. He held them both for some time. Maybe an onlooker would see a man considering what to do, maybe waiting for a sign.

Finally in a voice not his own, Eustice Seeney, the once King of the Underworld, said one word: "Ha."

It must have struck a chord as his body shook, then became rigid. And he hurled the rifle from its barrel so it flew end over end in an arc across the water. It seemed to float across the sky forever. As the silence was if all the sounds had been shut off in a recording studio. Finally it landed, breaking the water's surface like a bowling ball on an ice pond. The water shattered like crystal, and steam emerged and sizzled. A puff of red smoke floated up vertically, gradually dispersing in the morning sky. Eustice ran his thumb and fingers along the hat's brim, snorted, shook his head, and like a discus thrower mustered up all he had and hurled it across the water. It bounced a few times on the waters surface like a skipping rock, finally coming to rest a dozen or so yards away. Seconds after, it came to a stop. There were a few bubbles, then a whipping tail of a gator. A one eyed, twelve foot beast. In a fluid almost orchestration of something he'd seen on Animal Kingdom, the hat was in the jaws of the bull gator. Seeney would forever swear that critter looked right at him before he chomped down on it, and the hat went back into the food chain.

Without preamble he said, "It'll be a real hoot tryin' to poop out that Stetson you big dummy." Seeney walked over to his neighbor, felt for a pulse, and said: "Take it easy there good buddy, someone must've heard the shots and called 911." At that moment, despite the cloudless sky, it began to rain, and in the distance the sound of sirens grew louder.